——— THE ———
GRAND CANYON'S
UNCLE JIMMY
OWENS

——— THE ———
GRAND CANYON'S UNCLE JIMMY OWENS

ALBERT L. LeCount

THE
History
PRESS

Published by The History Press
Charleston, SC
www.historypress.com

Front cover, bottom: View of the Grand Canyon. *Photo by M. Quinn, National Park Service.*

First published 2021

ISBN 9781540246356

Library of Congress Control Number: 2020948631

Never throughout history has a man who lived a life of ease
left a name worth remembering
—Theodore Roosevelt

CONTENTS

FOREWORD

Al LeCount has performed an important service in compiling this Jim Owens biography. Unlike many of the noted or notorious men of the Southwest, Uncle Jimmy Owens was not a vicious outlaw or gun-slinging lawman accumulating notches on his gun. He was not a self-promoter, and in fact might not have been known at all had he not partnered with the outgoing and boisterous Buffalo Jones, and then been discovered by such worthies as Theodore Roosevelt, Zane Grey and Rex Beach. A quiet loner, Uncle Jim probably would have been happy to live in obscurity, working his bison herd or following Ranger, Pot and his other hounds alone on the Kaibab Plateau. Harold Pratt, game ranger on the North Kaibab during the 1950s through 1980, remembered Uncle Jimmy as a kindly soul who loved children—truly an "Uncle Jimmy."

Because the people who heralded him in books and articles were wealthy sportsmen, Owens's fame was centered on hunting mountain lions on the Kaibab Plateau. He and other less-known hunters and trappers reduced the population of large carnivores on the plateau to the point that the mule deer in the area experienced what is now the most famous irruption of a big game species in recorded history. This case of mismanagement of predators and deer has appeared in every wildlife management textbook since Aldo Leopold heralded it in his 1933 *Game Management*. Owens's prowess as a lion hunter contributed disproportionately to that irruption. With logging and grazing managed by the U.S. Forest Service, much of the North Rim protected by the U.S. Park Service and the mule deer managed by Arizona

Game and Fish Department, the plateau recovered and remains one of the best-known producers of trophy mule deer in America. Owens's impact on the lion and deer population was significant but temporary. His more lasting legacy was herding bison into Arizona. At the time that American bison were nearing extinction due to excessive hunting that had been encouraged by a U.S. government trying to eliminate the species as a food supply for Plains Indians, Owens and his partner, Buffalo Jones, shipped small herds of bison by rail into Utah and then accomplished the seemingly impossible by trail herding them to the North Kaibab Plateau. The descendants of those bison remain on the plateau today and have been used to create one other successful herd southeast of Flagstaff. Both of these herds are managed by Arizona Game and Fish Department.

But Owens had an earlier history. In a sense, he was one of several men who, during the late 1800s and the early 1900s, replaced the mountain man. Owens was the consummate man of the American West: born near San Antonio, Texas; leaving home as a boy, perhaps as young as eleven years of age; and doing a man's job on Charles Goodnight's ranch in the breaks of the Llano Estacado. It was while working for Goodnight that Owens learned to work with bison. It was also about this time that he was discovered by Buffalo Jones, the acquaintance who took Owens to Yellowstone Park and then to the North Kaibab Plateau. Jones was the more picturesque personality of the two and often appeared as a protagonist in books and articles of the time. However, if one reads carefully between the lines, Owens comes out as the quietly competent member of the partnership—the houndsman and hunter. He was also the stayer, while Jones constantly moved on to some new and sensational enterprise.

While assessing Uncle Jimmy's role as a lion hunter and guide, LeCount has fleshed out much of the younger Jim Owens's early history. He has also revealed connections between Owens and the Vaughns and Coxes, families who live, work and hunt on the Kaibab Plateau to this day. Based on modern land and wildlife management sciences, we might find much to criticize about Owens's activities. It is unfortunate, I suggest, that the literature of the nineteenth-century American West is flooded with Indian wars and gunfights, a literature that emphasizes brief but sensational events that create a false illusion of the times. The quiet and steadfast achievers like Owens, who had lasting effects, are too often distorted or ignored. LeCount has done a lot here to set the record straight.

—Harley G. Shaw

PREFACE

When most people think of the Grand Canyon National Park, they envision the South Rim, which receives over six million visitors a year. Few people realize that there is a second part to the park on the north side of the canyon, known as the North Rim. Only about 10 percent of park visitors ever make their way to the North Rim because of the long drive required to get there and the lack of the many tourist facilities found on the South Rim. Those who do, however, are treated to an area as wild and uninhabited as it was in the early 1900s. The North Rim is where Uncle Jimmy Owens lived and worked for over twenty years, tending his buffalo herd, hunting mountain lions and guiding early tourists on hunts and scenic trips.

I first became interested in Uncle Jimmy Owens because of work I had done on the North Rim as an employee for the Arizona Game and Fish Department. I've had the opportunity to hike and ride horseback over the same areas as Owens. I've hiked to the bottom of the canyon, floated the Colorado River and seen Thunder River pouring out of the canyon wall. I have also participated in hunts for descendants of Uncle Jimmy's buffalo, which he helped introduce to the area in 1906. Of course, I never had a chance to hunt with Owens, since he died long before I was born, but I have had a chance to experience what hunting mountain lions with hounds was like. Thanks to my good friends Dale and Clell Lee and Bill Workman, all of whom hunted lions with hounds the same as Owens, I have had an opportunity to experience lion hunts on many occasions. These hunts have given me a good feel for what it was like to hunt with Uncle Jimmy.

Writing this book has been a labor of love. Over a ten-year period, I have searched records, talked to individuals and read numerous articles about Owens. In some cases, facts about his life were found to be true, like comments made by people who knew him well, while others, such as his obituary, were found to be false. Some individuals who have read other articles about Owens might feel that I have left out some parts of his life, such as his wild drunken night when he put bullet holes in El Tovar Lodge on the South Rim of the canyon. I have chosen to not repeat such stories, since they could not be verified, and it's questionable if they really occurred.

To some readers, it might also appear that, in some places, this is more of a story of Buffalo Jones than Uncle Jimmy Owens. This is due to the fact that, starting when Jones first met Owens at the Goodnight Ranch in Texas in 1897–98, these two individuals' lives were intertwined until Jones left for New Mexico in 1909. It is impossible to document Owens's life without talking about Jones.

Another thing that some readers might question are the North Rim deer numbers I have presented. For those unfamiliar with estimating wildlife population numbers, they are simply approximations, not hard facts. The estimates I have presented were made by people who worked in the area during Owens's time and are based on whether they saw more or less deer than the year before. In other words, these estimates are nothing more than best guesses by the people who were there.

Some of the terminology I have used also needs explaining. Even though *bison* is the proper name for the animal, I have used the term *buffalo* because that was the common name used in Owens's time. I have also referred to the big cats that Owens pursued as mountain lions because that is the term commonly used in the West, even though in other areas they are referred to as cougars, pumas, catamounts, panthers and other names.

Some clarification is needed on the terminology used for the North Rim area where Owens lived and hunted. Technically, the entire area, including National Park Service, United States Forest Service and Bureau of Land Management lands, is known as the Kaibab Plateau or Kaibab. If one is talking of only National Forest Lands on the Kaibab Plateau, it is known as the North Kaibab Forest. National Park land on the north side of the Grand Canyon is commonly called the North Rim. Since Owens hunted in all of these areas, oftentimes in a single hunt, I have chosen to use the names interchangeably.

To give one a feeling for what it was like to pursue mountain lions in the cliffs and canyons of the North Rim, I have included several stories of

Owens's adventures. Although these stories might seem exaggerated, they are not. The instances were observed by people who were with him at the time. There are other stories I have chosen to leave out, however, since it is highly probable that they didn't really happen. One example is when Owens supposedly jumped off a small bank and landed astride a lion that was feeding on a deer carcass. The lion took off with Owens riding on its back for fifty or sixty feet before he fell off. Having had a similar experience, I believe this story has probably been embellished. In my case, I was hiking down a steep slope, jumping from one small ledge to another. As I started one jump, I looked down to see a lion lying on the next ledge about six feet below me. I thought I was going to land right on the cat's back, but before I hit the ground, he was up and gone. Due to the speed of a cat, there was no way I could have landed on it. Owens likely didn't either. It's a nice story to tell but probably didn't happen.

Owens is known to most people as a lion hunter, but he was much more. He was a cowboy, buffalo owner, guide and entrepreneur. In my writings, I have tried to present each aspect of Owens's life and the environment he lived in as accurately as possible. Hopefully, by the time you finish reading my work, you will know and appreciate the man, Uncle Jimmy Owens, a legend of the Grand Canyon.

—Al LeCount

ACKNOWLEDGEMENTS

Attempting to write a biography of a historical figure such as Uncle Jimmy Owens cannot be done alone. It involves hours of library research, along with correspondence with people, libraries and agencies, to compile a collection consisting of information relating to the individual. Computer searches have made some things easier, such as census records and voter registrations, but a great deal of time is still necessary to obtain information through visits to cemeteries and locations on the North Rim of the Grand Canyon, where Jimmy Owens's story takes place.

A very special thanks goes to my friend and colleague Harley Shaw. Harley not only took time to review a draft of the manuscript, but he was also more than willing to write the Foreword for this book. In addition, he took the time to locate what was left of the little town of Afton, New Mexico, where Owens lived out his final days. Harley also traveled to Las Cruces, New Mexico, to locate Owens's grave. Working with Carole Luke of the Masonic Cemetery in Las Cruces, he discovered that Owens was buried in an unmarked grave. Harley was also the one who suggested contacting retired Arizona Game and Fish employees to collect money to buy a tombstone to mark Owens's grave. I appreciate the contributions made by Wayne and Connie Anderson, Ray Kohls, Bob Barsch, Mike and Carol Godwin, Art Fuller, Matt and Clare Pierce, Lisa Anderson, Tom and Roxanne Britt, Cheryl Mollohan, Don and Jeanne Neff, Harley Shaw and Patty Woodruff, who gave willingly. They cannot be thanked enough for their donations, which provided a tombstone for Owens's final resting place.

ACKNOWLEDGEMENTS

I'm also very grateful to the employees of the United States Park Service for providing information on Owens, especially Colleen Hyde at Grand Canyon National Park. Colleen was invaluable in helping me look through all of the Grand Canyon National Park files on Owens. She also took the time to copy and mail me prints of important records, letters and photographs of Owens contained in the park's holdings. Similarly, I want to thank Ann Foster of Yellowstone National Park. Some of the material on Owens in Yellowstone's holdings were contained in bound volumes that were too fragile to copy, so she took the time to hand copy the information and send it to me. I really appreciate her efforts. Thanks also goes to the Cline Library at Northern Arizona University and the Panhandle-Plains Historical Museum Research Center in Canyon, Texas. Both provided me with copies of photographs from their collections.

Also, I want to thank Dick Brown. Dick has done extensive research on Buffalo Jones and willingly shared any information he found on Owens. Dick found some historic papers that I might have missed if it had not been for his generous sharing and encouragement on this project. Mary Gilbert's editing ability helped find many typos and punctuation and wording errors that I missed in the manuscript and made the text much more readable. I appreciate her help. I am also indebted to Tom Britt and Ron Smith, both retired from the Arizona Game and Fish Department, who gave me their best guesses on the number of deer on the Kaibab Plateau at various times. Unfortunately, Ron died before this project was completed.

A special thanks also goes to Leon Cox of Orderville, Utah, for sharing his collection of magazines and newspaper clippings on Owens. When I told Leon that I was going to try to write a book on Uncle Jimmy Owens, he immediately sent me all of the material he had collected on Owens over many years. It was in Leon's material that I discovered the only actual interview of Owens, which was done for an article in the 1937 issue of *Field and Stream* magazine. Leon's material also gave me the connection to the Owens family in Eastland, Texas. Other good insights to Owens's life as a hunter and buffalo manager were also obtained from books by authors such as Robert Easton and Mackenzie Brown, *Lord of Beasts: The Saga of Buffalo Jones*; Theodore Roosevelt, *A Book Lover's Holiday*; and Rex Beach, *Oh, Shoot! Confessions of an Agitated Sportsman*.

I am also deeply indebted to Laurie Krill of The History Press. Laurie saw that there was a story that needed to be told about Uncle Jimmy Owens. Her help and encouragement are what got his story published. She was always there to answer questions and give help where it was needed. Without her, this book would not have happened.

Finally, I want to thank my wife, Cheryl Mollohan, who put up with me pursuing Owens's history for over ten years. She traveled with me to the Grand Canyon, which for her was also a labor of love, since the North Rim is one of her favorite places in Arizona. Together we looked at various sites and locations used by Owens. She also helped read many of the National Park Service's historic documents, deciding which were important to the project. Her comments on the project were irreplaceable. I couldn't have done it without her love and encouragement.

INTRODUCTION

If you happen to travel to the North Rim of the Grand Canyon, you will find a sign pointing to the start of the North Kaibab Trail, which travels down Bright Angel Creek to the Colorado River. Near that sign, you will find another sign marking the beginning of the Uncle Jim Trail, which leads to Uncle Jim Point, but there is no explanation about who Uncle Jim was or why he had a trail named after him. A search of the internet informs that in 1932 the National Board of Geographic Names renamed Nachi Point and the trail to it in honor of Uncle Jimmy Owens, who, among other things, killed over four hundred mountain lions to protect the deer on the North Rim.[1] Lumping the rest of this man's life into "among other things," however, does not begin to tell his story. For over twenty years (1906–29), Owens called the North Rim home. He hunted mountain lions, first as a game warden with the United States Forest Service and later as an independent guide. He was also instrumental in bringing the first buffalo to the North Rim and managed the herd for many years. His lifestyle, and the North Rim of the Grand Canyon where he lived, fascinated such authors as Zane Grey and Marguerite Henry, both of whom used him as a character in their books.

If you happened to meet James T. Owens, better known as Uncle Jimmy, riding his horse or mule among the pines on the North Rim, he would appear much like any cowboy of the late 1800s or early 1900s. He wore a broad-brimmed hat, a wool shirt, suspenders to hold up his Levi pants and a pair of good hiking boots. On his waist was a cartridge belt and a .45 pistol.

Uncle Jim Trailhead near Grand Canyon's North Rim Visitor Center. *Photo by A. LeCount.*

On his saddle he carried a .30-.30 carbine. He was a small, wiry-built man, standing about five foot seven and weighing about 170 pounds. His hair was gray, as was his small mustache. Owens never married and had no children of his own but had several nephews, Bob and Bill Vaughn and Ed Cox, who lived and hunted with him at various times. There were stories of him being an outlaw, shooting a man and riding with gangs, but these appear to be just stories. In fact, just the opposite appears to be the case. Bill Mace, a forest ranger who knew Owens for many years, described him as "a quiet and gentle man with a quiet dignity and personality that made him friends of everyone. If anyone stopped by his camp, they were treated as a friend and were well fed and taken care of. He would have been rated as a good neighbor in any country."[2]

Ben Swapp, another Kaibab Forest ranger who knew Owens well, said, "He was just a good clean man who he never heard an unkind word from or about him."[3] This quiet demeanor, however, masked his underlying character. He was also said to be fearless. He thought nothing of climbing on small ledges or cliffs in pursuit of a lion, where a misstep would mean

View of the Grand Canyon from Uncle Jim Point. *Photo by A. LeCount.*

a plunge of hundreds or thousands of feet to his death. He was also quick to act if he thought a person or one of his hounds was in danger, with no thought of any danger to himself. The one thing that was different when you met Owens was that, since his job was to hunt mountain lions, he was always accompanied by a pack of hounds. He pursued hundreds of these big cats by himself for over twenty years, often camped out in the rain, cold and snow. Many times, he risked his life as he descended over the rim of the Grand Canyon in pursuit of one of the big cats.

For those unfamiliar with mountain lions, they are large cats. They occur throughout the western United States and are common throughout the Southwest. Males measure five to nine feet in length and weigh 150 to 200 pounds. Females are smaller, weighing 80 to 130 pounds and averaging five to seven feet from head to tail. Lions are very mobile animals, covering as much as ninety to one hundred square miles in search of food. They hunt and kill some smaller animals, such as skunks, porcupines and rabbits, but their primary prey are deer. Lions, like all cats, are very agile and are capable of jumping ten to fifteen feet up ledges, cliffs and trees. They

Uncle Jim Owens on the North Rim in 1920. *Northern Arizona University Library, NAU ph.165.1.*

are also fast for a short distance when catching prey but cannot run long distances, which is why hunters like Owens could catch them with a pack of hounds.[4]

Uncle Jimmy lived and worked on the North Rim of the Grand Canyon and north to the Arizona-Utah border. In Owens's time, it took days to reach this area. Roads, where they occurred, were nothing more than rutted wagon roads. The nearest rail access from the north was at Lund Utah, 170 miles away. A spur line of the Santa Fe railroad extended to El Tovar Lodge on the South Rim of the Grand Canyon, but then one had to cross the canyon on steep narrow trails and cross the dangerous Colorado River to reach the other side. Even today, fewer than 10 percent of visitors to the Grand Canyon find their way to the North Rim.

The country north of the Grand Canyon was first settled by Mormon pioneers who established both cattle and sheep operations in the area. However, due to winter snows, few people established permanent residences near the canyon rim, preferring to live at lower elevations in Fredonia, Arizona, and Kanab, Utah. These two towns are still occupied by those individuals who work on the North Rim, for there are no other close towns in this remote country.

The North Rim country encompasses a large plateau originally known as Buckskin Mountain. This area was home to a large mule deer herd that the Southern Paiute Indians traditionally hunted for hides to make into buckskin, which gave the mountain its name. Today, the area is generally known as the Kaibab Plateau, or just the Kaibab, which means "mountain lying down."[5]

Seen from a distance, the Kaibab does resemble a flat-topped mountain. It is a large plateau, extending sixty miles from just south of Fredonia, Arizona, to the North Rim of the Grand Canyon, and is forty-five miles wide at its widest point. This plateau rises from approximately five thousand feet on the north end to a little over nine thousand feet at the rim of the canyon, which is one thousand feet higher than the South Rim.[6] To the north, the terrain gradually descends toward the Arizona-Utah border, while the east and west sides drop off sharply into cliffs and deeply eroded canyons. The south end of the plateau ends abruptly at the rim of the Grand Canyon.

Vegetation varies from sagebrush, juniper and pinyon pine at the lower elevations to ponderosa pine and a mixture of spruce and fir trees covering most of the higher elevations. Interspersed throughout the forest are small and large grassy meadows, commonly referred to as parks. Deer, and the predators that follow them, use these parks and forested areas on the plateau

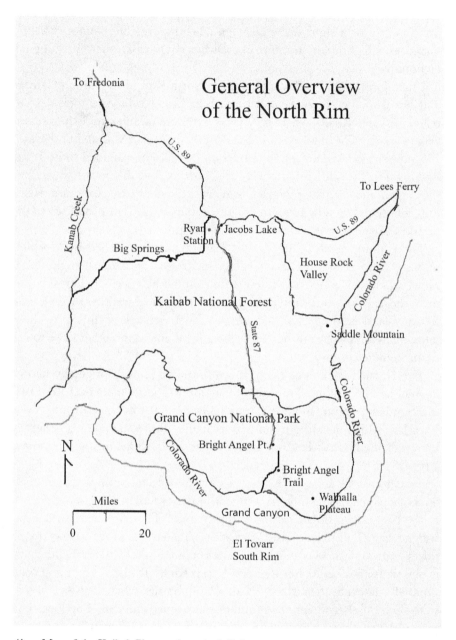

Above: Map of the Kaibab Plateau. *Image by A. LeCount.*

Opposite: Bright Angel Point on the southern edge of the Kaibab Plateau plunges into the Grand Canyon. *Grand Canyon National Park Museum Collection, no. 05439.*

during the summer months and then move to the lower tablelands on the east and west sides when the snow covers the higher elevations.

On the Kaibab Plateau, summer temperatures are warm, accompanied by frequent thunderstorms. In the winter, snow can reach four to eight feet at the higher elevations near the canyon rim. During the summer months, Owens and his hounds could be found hunting from his cabin in Harvey Meadow, near the head of Bright Angel Creek. In winter, he camped out and hunted where there was less snow or stayed at one of several ranches in the area. One of his favorite camping spots east of the plateau was a cave with a large boulder shaped like a house not far from the Arizona-Utah border, which gave the area its name, House Rock Valley. Owens liked this place because twice a week the mail carrier would come by and he would have someone to visit with. When he was hunting west of the plateau, he liked to stay in a cabin on Jump Up Point.[7]

Even though the North Rim was remote, Owens attracted the interest of individuals who wanted to hunt a mountain lion, capture one alive or just see one. Since Owens's job was to kill lions, the Forest Service had no problem with him taking people along on his hunts as a paid guide. Some individuals attracted to his skills included the rich and famous, such as writer Zane Grey and the avid hunter who got Owens his job on the North Rim, President Theodore Roosevelt. His exploits also attracted the attention of people who had no desire to kill a mountain lion but were fascinated by Owens's lifestyle. One such individual was Marguerite Henry, who used him as the somewhat fictitious character Uncle Jim in her book *Brighty of the Grand Canyon*.

Along with hunting mountain lions, buffalo also were an important part of Owens's life. While working on the Goodnight Ranch in Texas, he met Charles "Buffalo" Jones, who wanted to experiment crossing buffalo with domestic cattle, producing an animal called a cattalo or beefalo. It was believed that this cross would be much more adapted to cold winters than pure cattle breeds and would have a good market value. While both Jones and Owens were working at Yellowstone National Park, they discussed the possibility of starting a cattalo ranch somewhere. The question was where. One area they discussed was the remote country in northern Arizona and southeastern Utah. To see if this area had potential for their ranch, Jones, in 1904, took leave from his job as buffalo warden in Yellowstone and visited the Kaibab. To his delight, Jones found the area as the ideal place for their cattalo project. As a result, they introduced buffalo to the North Rim in 1906. Unfortunately, after several breeding seasons, it became obvious that trying to cross buffalo and cattle wasn't going to work. Jones soon lost interest in the project, and he and the other investors dropped out one by one. Eventually, Owens became the sole owner of the herd, and in 1927, he sold it to the State of Arizona.

Owens remained on the North Rim until 1929. With his health failing and plagued by something all hunters who follow a pack of hounds fear, a loss of hearing, Owens left the Kaibab Plateau. The story doesn't end there, because he not only left the Kaibab, but he also completely disappeared. Searches were made for his grave at all of the cemeteries in northern Arizona and southern Utah to no avail. It took obtaining his death certificate to find that he was supposedly buried in the Masonic Cemetery in Las Cruces, New Mexico, far from his beloved Kaibab. However, a search of tombstone records at the cemetery did not show him to be buried there. It was only through the generous help of cemetery worker Carole Luke that his final resting place was found.

1

TEXAS, THE EARLY YEARS

Little is known about the Owens family. In the 1910 census, Jimmy stated that his father was born in Pennsylvania and his mother in Illinois.[8] When the family arrived in Texas is not known, but by the 1830s, the family was in the San Antonio area, where James Thos Owens was probably born. This fact is substantiated by Teddy Roosevelt, who on a hunting trip with Owens asked him where he was born. Owens replied San Antonio.[9] However, when he was born is confusing.

When Uncle Jimmy Owens died on May 11, 1936, his obituary and death certificate stated that he was born in San Antonio, Texas, on April 10, 1836, making him one hundred years old at the time of his death. It also stated that his parents were killed at the Alamo, which appears to not be the case.[10] There is no record of any Owens, either civilian or military, at the Alamo. In addition, the Battle of the Alamo occurred from February 23 through March 6, 1836, making it unlikely that he was born in April 1836. Unfortunately, the only portion of his obituary that appears to be true is that he was born in or near San Antonio.[11] Why the author of the obituary and death certificate chose to embellish Owens's life to make him one hundred years old is not known.

If Owens was not born in April 1836, just when was he born? A check of census records makes one wonder if Owens even knew when he was born. He managed to avoid the census takers until the 1910 Arizona census, probably because he was living in remote areas and moved several times. In 1910, when he was first recorded in the Arizona census, he stated that he was born in 1861.[12] In the 1920 census, he failed to state his birth date, but in the 1930 census, he said he was born in 1848.[13] A third birth date of 1857 was given in an article by Annie Dyer Nunn, who knew Owens personally.[14] When Annie was a young girl, Owens came to work for her father. Undoubtedly, they visited and discussed such things as birthdays, but the 1857 date might also be incorrect. At a later date, Nunn stated that Owens was born in 1849.[15] Based on the various birth dates, one can probably only say that Owens was born in the late 1850s or early 1860s, making him in his eighties at the time of his death.

How many children Owens's parents had is also unknown, but it appears he had several sisters. In the 1920 census, when asked who else resided in his residence, he listed a William Vaughn, adopted son.[16] It seems unlikely that he would have listed a complete stranger as adopted. It would also explain why he was always known as uncle Jimmy Owens. William Vaughn and his brother, Bob, were born and raised in Claude, Texas, and eventually traveled to the North Rim to hunt with their Uncle Jim. Bill Vaughn was killed in World War I, but as Owens grew older, Bob took over more and more of the hunting and eventually inherited some of Jim's hounds. Bob continued to

Claude Texas. Home of Owens's nephews Bill and Bob Vaughn and near the Goodnight ranch, where Owens worked. *Leon Cox.*

guide lion hunts, primarily in southern Utah, for many years after his uncle left the North Rim.[17]

In later life, when Owens moved to New Mexico, he lived with another nephew, John Cox.[18] The Cox family appears to have hailed from Eastland, Texas, where Uncle Jimmy had two more nephews, Ed and John Cox. Ed eventually moved to the Kaibab and lived with his uncle Jim, helping with lion hunts and buffalo herding. Some Vaughns and Coxes still reside north of the Grand Canyon.[19]

Owens's father died when Jim was a young child, but his mother soon remarried. It might have been then that some or all of the family moved to Claude, Texas. Young Jim did not get along with his new stepfather, so at the age of eleven, he ran away from home and joined a cattle drive, beginning his career as a cowboy.[20] Like many ranch hands of his day, Owens worked for a variety of ranches in Oklahoma and Texas. It was during this time that several stories about Owens occurred. One was that he rode with the Jesse James gang and another was that he once killed a man. Both, however, appear to be unsubstantiated and probably did not occur. A check of the various members of the James Gang shows that no Owens was ever recorded as a member. Also, while Owens was working on ranches in Texas and Oklahoma, the James Gang was doing most of its robbing in Missouri and in other states to the north and east. The story of his killing a man also seems doubtful, since he did not try to leave the area for fear of being arrested. In fact, for over thirty years, he remained in the Texas Panhandle, only leaving later in life to take a job at Yellowstone National Park.

In 1876, a prominent cattleman named Charles Goodnight changed the direction of Owens's life. Goodnight, in partnership with an Irishman, John G. Adair, established the JA Ranch, the first permanent ranch in Palo Duro Canyon in the Texas Panhandle. Eventually, the ranch encompassed over 1 million acres and had over 100,000 cattle.[21] Owens went to work for Goodnight, and for the next thirty years, he was employed either by Charles Goodnight or by Goodnight's brothers-in-law Lee and Walter Dyer, who also had ranches in the area.[22] Although Goodnight had a big effect on Owens's life, he wasn't alone. Another Goodnight, Mary Ann, Charles's wife, also played an important role in Owens's future.

Texas rancher Charles Goodnight, who hired young Jimmy Owens and eventually promoted him to foremen of his ranch. *Wikimedia Commons.*

Palo Duro Canyon, where Goodnight established his ranch, is much like the north end of the Kaibab Plateau. The area is steep and rough with many deep canyons and ravines. Juniper and sagebrush are common in both areas. A variety of wildlife species are also found in both areas, including deer, wild turkeys, coyotes and, in Owens's time, mountain lions. Since these big cats prey on not only deer but also cattle, it was probably in Palo Duro Canyon where Owens first learned to use hounds to pursue and kill lions that were killing livestock.

When Goodnight first brought his cattle to Palo Duro Canyon, Jimmy Owens was one of the drovers, along with Lee, Sam and Walter Dyer, younger brothers of Mary Ann. As they drove the herd into the canyon, it was full of buffalo, which had to be driven out because they would compete with the cattle for food. Whenever a buffalo herd reentered the canyon, it was the cowboys' job to drive them back out. Since the sides of the canyon were steep and rugged, many calves were left behind. To prevent these calves from starving, Goodnight instructed his cowboys to kill them. At first, Mary Ann didn't know this was happening, but when she found out, she put a stop to it. She realized that buffalo were rapidly disappearing due to hide hunters, who killed thousands, and a concerted effort by the U.S. government to ensure the defeat of Native Americans by eliminating their food supply. To do her part to stop this decline, she wanted these orphan calves brought to the ranch to be taken care of before buffalo disappeared from the Great Plains. Charles Goodnight was always given credit for saving some of the last buffalo in the Texas Panhandle, but he was quick to point out that it was really his wife, Mary Ann, who initiated the idea.

It wasn't just Mary Ann who realized buffalo were being eliminated at a rapid rate. Both Charles Goodnight and Jimmy Owens also realized that if something wasn't done buffalo would disappear. By the mid-1870s, Goodnight estimated that there were three thousand buffalo hunters in the Texas Panhandle, and Owens once stated that over a two-year period he always heard gunshots as hide hunters eliminated the

Charles Goodnight gets credit for helping save buffalo from extinction, but it was his wife, Mary Ann "Molly" Goodnight, who pushed to save orphaned buffalo calves and start a captive herd on their ranch. *Panhandle-Plains Historical Society.*

buffalo herds.[23] As he rode the range working cattle, Owens also undoubtedly experienced what a rancher by the name of Theodore Roosevelt experienced in the Dakota Territory at about the same time. Roosevelt stated:

> *No sight is more common on the plains than that of a bleached buffalo skull, and their countless numbers attest to the abundance of the animal at a time not very long past. On those portions where the herds made their last stand the carcasses dried in the clear, high air, or the moldering skeletons abound. Last year in crossing the country around the heads of the Big Sandy, O'Fallon Creek, Little Beaver and Box Elder, these skeletons or dried carcasses were in sight from every hillock, often lying over the ground so thickly that several score could be seen at once.*

Roosevelt also noted that he had talked to another rancher who told him he had ridden one thousand miles across northern Montana and was never out of sight of buffalo bones and never in sight of a buffalo.[24] Owens undoubtedly saw the same thing on the ranges in Texas.

Following his wife's suggestion, Goodnight decided to start his own private buffalo herd. Being around buffalo on a daily basis, Goodnight observed that if a herd was chased, the young calves would not be able to keep up. Feeling lost after their mothers were gone, they would follow his horse, and he could lead them back to his ranch. There, he would put them in with domestic cows that would allow them to nurse. Goodnight's buffalo project started out slow, since the great herds were almost gone, and it was increasingly difficult to find the remaining herds. In his first year, he only captured four calves, but the next year, he added twenty to his herd. Over the next twenty years, Owens saw the Goodnight herd grow into one of the largest in the United States, and Owens spent a lot of his time working and managing buffalo, along with cattle.[25] It was while working for Goodnight that Owens met another person who was also trying to save the buffalo and who would have a big influence on his life, Charles "Buffalo" Jones.

Jones was originally a buffalo hunter, killing thousands of the animals, but like Goodnight, he became alarmed that if the killing continued buffalo could become extinct. To prevent this from happening, Jones started forming his own herd by capturing wild buffalo calves in the Texas Panhandle in 1886.[26] To get his calves, though, he used a different technique than Goodnight. When Jones, always a flamboyant character, located a herd, he would pursue it at full speed, and when he was close enough to a calf, he would rope it, jump off his horse and tie its feet together so it couldn't run off. He would then jump back on his horse and pursue another calf. Once he was done, the calves were loaded into a wagon and taken to his ranch in Garden City, Kansas.[27] In addition to capturing his own calves, he also purchased some animals from ranchers in Canada, Kansas, Nebraska and Texas. One such rancher was Charles Goodnight.

As various ranchers were forming their buffalo herds, they started to look at ways to make a profit from their animals. Some sold buffalo to zoos, parks and individuals who wanted to start a buffalo herd. Others charged for viewing buffalo, and some even experimented with spinning buffalo hair into yarn. A few also tried to turn some of them into work animals. One such individual was Jones.[28]

In 1897 or 1898, Jones traveled from his home in Garden City, Kansas, to Goodnight's ranch to buy a couple of buffalo that he wanted to teach to pull a sled for exhibition purposes. By this time, Goodnight had promoted Jimmy Owens to foreman, so it was Owens who was assigned to help Jones get his buffalo trained. They soon found, however, that training buffalo to work was not as easy as training oxen. After working for days, Owens said, "We got them gentle enough to drive if you could call it that." To train them, the buffalo were yoked to a sled that had a windlass with a rope attached to their

Buffalo Jones driving a team of buffalo that Owens helped him train to pull a cart while at the Goodnight Ranch. *Panhandle-Plains Historical Society.*

front feet for controlling the team. Jones would stop the team by giving the windlass a few cranks, which would jerk the buffalo to their knees. To start them again, he would slack the rope on the windlass. According to Owens, "It was as simple as that."[29] Jones's buffalo show proved very successful, until his animals died from the heat in Fort Worth, Texas. But by working together, Owens and Jones struck up a friendship that lasted for many years.

Jones's buffalo show was not the only venture that he tried with buffalo. Both he and Goodnight attempted breeding buffalo with cattle to produce a hybrid called a cattalo. They hoped that this cross would produce an animal that was more adapted to the harsh winters of the plains than regular cattle. Being the ranch foreman, Owens was part of all of Goodnight's buffalo projects, including his cattalo project. He learned how to handle and work with buffalo and observed Goodnight's attempts to produce cattalo—something Owens and Jones would try in the future.

YELLOWSTONE BUFFALO WARDEN

Buffalo were native to the Yellowstone area, and by 1872, when President Ulysses S. Grant created the 3,500-square-mile Yellowstone National Park, the area supported four to five hundred buffalo. Although nowhere near the thousands that historically roamed the prairies, this was the largest herd left in the United States. Creation of the park technically prohibited any destruction of fish and game, including buffalo, but Congress provided no money to operate the park. For the first five years, Yellowstone had no money for roads, and the administrative personnel, including the superintendent, received no salary. There was also no one to help protect wildlife. Consequently, the area was attractive to poachers and vandals, who took advantage of the situation. By 1875, the hide hunters had reduced Yellowstone's buffalo to a point that they were difficult to find. Things became so bad that in 1876 the United States cavalry relieved the civilian superintendent of his duties and took over the job as park police.[30]

With the park under army protection, soldiers would remove any individuals they found hunting or vandalizing the area. Their actions greatly reduced poaching, but because there was no fine or imprisonment if they got caught, some individuals still took the risk to enter the park and shoot buffalo. On a visit to the newly established Yellowstone National Park in 1875, naturalist George Grinnell noted that many buffalo were still being poached and something more had to be done to protect what buffalo were left.[31] In Washington, D.C., Congress finally agreed that the only way to stop the killing of buffalo in Yellowstone was through legislation.

Yellowstone National Park was established in 1872, but poaching of buffalo like these continued until it was estimated that there were only twenty-five left in the park by 1894. *Yellowstone National Park, no. 16058.*

In 1894, Congress passed the National Park Protection Act. This bill had provisions for a jail sentence of up to two years and fines as high as $1,000 for anyone caught killing game in Yellowstone. The only problem was that the legislation came twenty years too late. Park officials had always estimated the number of buffalo in the park from four to five hundred animals, but in 1894, when Commanding Officer George Anderson surveyed the herd, he found only about twenty-five animals. Twenty years of so-called protection by the army had resulted in the poaching of nearly five hundred animals.[32]

When word of the buffalo situation in Yellowstone Park got back to Washington, people began to get concerned. One such individual was President Theodore Roosevelt. Having ranched in the Dakotas, Roosevelt had seen the elimination of buffalo from the Badlands. He realized that if the Yellowstone herd was to be saved, it would take an individual who understood these animals. That individual was Buffalo Jones.

Jones had gained a great deal of notoriety for capturing animals alive from a trip he made to the Arctic Circle to capture musk ox calves. Because of this ability, Jones was asked by the Smithsonian Institute to capture some Rocky Mountain bighorn sheep for the National Zoological Park.

This job took him to Washington, D.C., where he met with Theodore Roosevelt. Because both men were interested in buffalo, the conversation turned to how to protect what was left of the Yellowstone herd. Various options were considered, but it was finally decided that the only way to protect the remaining animals was to establish a captive herd in Yellowstone Park. In 1902, because of Jones's vast experience with buffalo, Roosevelt appointed him as the park's first game warden, with the primary duty of reestablishing buffalo in the park.[33]

At that time, Yellowstone was being operated by the United States cavalry, which treated it like a military base, although concessioners, such as Wylie Way, were allowed to operate their camps and hotels for tourists. Until this time, the army acted primarily as park police, capturing poachers if they happened to find them. With Jones's arrival as game warden in July 1902, all wildlife matters were turned over to him.[34]

To accomplish the task of creating a captive herd, Jones set out to construct a fenced area and stock it with some native buffalo. Because there was fear that the native herd might be inbred, he was to supplement it with animals from other herds. The site selected for this pen was near Mammoth Hot Springs. This was a strange choice since the native herd preferred other areas of the park, but the Mammoth Valley was a main entrance to the park, and people could visit the corrals to see buffalo.

The next step was to stock the pen with buffalo. To help with this task, Congress had appropriated $15,000 for the purchase of buffalo. Jones got his animals from various herds. He purchased eighteen cows from a herd owned by Charles Allard in Montana.[35] Next, he headed to the Goodnight Ranch in Texas to obtain three bulls. When Jones visited the ranch to pick them up, he undoubtedly renewed his friendship with Goodnight's foreman, Jimmy Owens. While there, he probably also told Owens about his opportunity and plans for Yellowstone and its buffalo herd.

Part of Owens's job as buffalo keeper in Yellowstone was to take care of this herd near Mammoth Hot Springs. *Yellowstone National Park, no. 03007.*

On his return to Yellowstone, Jones set about trying to supplement his penned herd with animals from the wild herd. In the dead of winter, he set out to capture some wild calves by using his technique of chasing the herd until the calves dropped behind. The only difference was that he attempted to do it on skiis rather than a horse. As preposterous as it sounds, he was able to capture two calves and add them to his captured herd.[36]

Besides establishing a captive buffalo herd, Jones had other responsibilities as the park's game warden. One was dealing with bears that were at garbage dumps and tourist camps. To discourage them from visiting such areas, he handled the problem in his own unique way. He would rope the bear, string it up by one leg and proceed to whip it with a stick.[37] Owens learned this technique from Jones, and when he occasionally caught a bear on the Kaibab Plateau, he did the same thing.

During such operations as handling bears or other problem wildlife, the cavalry would send a trooper to assist Jones, but he found them to be of little help. They were untrained and inexperienced in handling wildlife. In his growing frustration with these individuals assigned to him, he wrote in a letter to park superintendent major John Pitcher, stating, "I have several times asked you to select someone who is an expert with a rope and all around good western man who would be in accord with me and not always finding fault, hoping thereby to have me discharged that they could get appointed game warden."[38]

The man Jones had in mind was Jimmy Owens from Texas. At some point, probably when he renewed his acquaintance with Owens at the Goodnight Ranch, Jones convinced Owens to come work with him as a buffalo keeper. Owens accepted the offer and moved to Yellowstone.

When Owens arrived at Yellowstone, he talked to Jones about starting a cattalo ranch somewhere. One area that interested them was the North Rim of the Grand Canyon. By 1904, their plans had become serious enough that Jones started making trips to the Grand Canyon area to find a suitable location. These trips seemed to aggravate Major John Pitcher, as Jones was not tending to his Yellowstone business. Pitcher and Jones had a history of confrontations, which came to a head when Jones suggested that the military was incapable of administering Yellowstone and should be replaced by civilians. In response, Pitcher wrote a letter to the secretary of interior, Hitchcock, accusing Jones of laziness, embezzlement and absenteeism, pointing out the fact that Jones was currently in Arizona, where he was making plans to establish a cattalo ranch. As a result of these accusations, and with a new opportunity, Jones resigned as buffalo keeper on December 27, 1904. On Jones's departure, Pitcher sent the following letter to the secretary of the interior:[39]

December 28ᵗʰ 1904
The Honorable E. A. Hitchcock
Secretary of the Interior,
Washington D.C.

Sir,

   Referring to letter from this office dated December 16ᵗʰ, 1904, forwarding vouchers for payment in favor of Mr. C.J. Jones as Buffalo Keeper in the Yellowstone National Park for part of the month of December, 1904 and stating that Mr. Jones had resigned, I have the honor to request authority to employ in his stead Mr. J.T. Owens, from and including December 27ᵗʰ, 1904 at the rate of $900.00 per annum, payable from the amount allotted for pay of Buffalo Keeper by Department letter dated June 28ᵗʰ, 1904 from appropriation for "Maintenance of Buffalo, 1905."

   Mr. Owens comes from Goodnight, Texas and he has had considerable experience with buffalo and comes well recommended, it is believed that he will prove a suitable man for the place.

Very respectfully
John Pitcher
Major 6ᵗʰ Cavalry
Acting Superintendent

Owens agreed and was hired as Yellowstone's buffalo keeper in 1904 for seventy-five dollars per month.[40] In his new job, he became responsible for not only buffalo but also all wildlife in Yellowstone. This included taking over a pack of hounds purchased by the park to kill mountain lions, something Owens probably knew something about from his experiences in Texas. Owens stayed on at Yellowstone until April 1906, when, at the request of Teddy Roosevelt, he became Arizona's first game warden on the newly created Grand Canyon Game Preserve. It was there that he would join Jones in their new venture, raising cattalo on the North Rim of the Grand Canyon.

   This appointment by Roosevelt came about in a mysterious way. While Uncle Jimmy was in the Yellowstone area, he had an opportunity to meet the president, however just when and how they met is something of a mystery. In 1903, President Roosevelt decided to make a tour of the western United

Roosevelt's friend naturalist John Burroughs traveled with Roosevelt when he toured Yellowstone. *Yellowstone National Park, no. 14514.*

States, stopping at the South Rim of the Grand Canyon and at Yellowstone National Park. Before his arrival, Yellowstone's superintendent, Major John Pitcher, wrote Roosevelt to tell him that mountain lions were eating all of the elk. Roosevelt was sympathetic to this problem and felt that if you could reduce mountain lion predation on deer and elk, it would help these populations recover. With this idea in mind, he planned to hunt lions while in Yellowstone. Word of this hunt was quickly picked up by the press, which depicted Roosevelt's trip as a private hunting trip in the park. To quell the rumors, he told Pitcher that on his tour of the park, he wanted only a small party that included Pitcher and Roosevelt's traveling companion, naturalist John Burroughs. He left behind his private secretaries, Secret Service agents and even his private physician. Before leaving, he stated to the press that he would abide by the park's rule and "not a gun would be fired within the Park," even though park officials were willing to waive their no hunting rule for the president.[41]

Whether Owens had an opportunity to meet Roosevelt on his Yellowstone tour is doubtful. He might not have arrived in Yellowstone before Roosevelt's visit, but if he was in the area, it appears that he wasn't part of Roosevelt's formal party. After the 1903 trip, both Roosevelt and his traveling companion, Burroughs, wrote about their travels through Yellowstone, but neither mentioned Owens.[42] However, there is the possibility that Owens could have met Roosevelt when the president visited the buffalo pens, which would have been where Owens worked. If such a meeting did occur, neither Roosevelt nor Owens ever mentioned it.

Mysteriously, though, in his later years, Owens mentioned a meeting with Roosevelt in 1904, a year after the president's visit to Yellowstone. He talked of a three-day hunt with Roosevelt that year. The encounter, as described by Owens, was a 1904 hunting trip on a ranch in Wyoming. Owens said that he and President Roosevelt happened to visit the same ranch in Wyoming at the same time and hunted together for three days.[43] However, Roosevelt,

Whether Charles M. Russell met Owens or just saw a picture of him is not known, but he produced this 1905 watercolor of Uncle Jimmy for a book titled *Arizona Nights. Stewart E. White, Arizona Nights, 1907.*

who wrote about most of his hunting trips, never mentioned a 1904 Wyoming hunt or any other hunt with Owens, until he hunted with him in Arizona in 1913. Was Owens mistaken about the date, did it never occur or did Roosevelt choose to not mention it in any of his writings? There is some evidence to substantiate Owens's story. About the same time, the famous Western artist Charles Russell also encountered Owens. Whether he actually met him in Yellowstone or somewhere in Wyoming is not known, but Russell was impressed enough with the mule rider and his hounds that he painted a picture of him.[44] Owens never mentioned meeting Russell, but could this have been when Owens said he hunted with Roosevelt? Even though it remains a mystery, it is obvious that Roosevelt and Owens did meet at some point and had time to get to know each other, because in 1906, Roosevelt made Owens the first game warden in the newly created Grand Canyon Game Preserve.

THE CATTALO PROJECT

W hile at Yellowstone, Jimmy Owens and Buffalo Jones shared their common interest in saving some of the last remaining buffalo and the possibility of using them to raise a crossbreed animal known as a *cattalo*. Buffalo Jones is credited with coining the word cattalo, but he was not the first to try buffalo-cattle crosses. When Europeans started to settle the eastern United States, small herds of buffalo were found throughout the Ohio Valley and south to the Carolinas.[45] By the early 1800s, a few individuals had tried crossing buffalo with cattle, producing a cattalo. Most of these endeavors were little more than small experiments, and it wasn't until the 1870s that a concerted effort was made to raise cattalo. In the 1870s, J.W. Cunningham of Howard County, Nebraska, started to raise a few buffalo with the intention of crossing them with his domestic cattle to obtain a heartier animal that could better stand the cold Nebraska winters. He was somewhat successful in getting heifers from the cross, which eventually gave birth to three-quarter bred calves. These hybrid animals were purchased by other ranchers, and eventually, a few crossbred animals extended throughout areas of Howard County.[46]

By the late 1800s, cattalo production had caught the interest of other ranchers throughout the Great Plains, including Charles Goodnight. What these individuals were hoping to get from these buffalo-cattle crosses was not only a hardier animal but also a larger animal that would produce more meat. Goodnight experimented with cattalo and found not only did they make a larger and hardier animal, but "they required less food, were a longer-lived animal, and would produce more net meat than any other cattle."[47] This description made cattalo sound like the ideal animal, except for several problems.

Breeders found that when crossing a buffalo bull with a domestic cow many cows died trying to produce a calf. Other cows often aborted bull calves or they were stillborn, and the bull calves that did survive proved to be sterile. These problems occurred regardless of the breed of cow. Trying to cross buffalo cows with a domestic bull also had its problems. The cross killed fewer cows and produced more bull calves, but in most cases buffalo cows disliked domestic bulls and avoided them. Goodnight concluded that the only way to get a buffalo cow to breed with a domestic bull was to raise the two together from birth.[48]

Similar results were found by Mossom Boyd in Ontario, Canada. Boyd made over one hundred successful crosses of domestic cows by buffalo bulls. Of those, two-thirds aborted, and of the remaining thirty-nine, six were males, and only two of these survived after twenty-four hours. Three others died before adulthood, and the remaining male was sterile.[49] In his twenty years of trying to raise cattalo, Boyd successfully raised thirty-three females and no males. He continued to experiment with cattalo for twenty years but failed to produce a viable cattalo herd.[50]

One of the biggest promoters of cattalo was Buffalo Jones, even though Boyd's work was cause for concern. He, like Goodnight, thought the hybrid would not only inherit the buffalo's ability to handle winter snow and cold better than cattle but that the animals would also be in great demand for their hides and meat. He thought one way to improve the survival was to breed them with black Galloway cattle, which had the ability to produce large calves.

In 1887, Jones started his cattalo experiment. He put two yearling and two two-year-old buffalo bulls in with his Galloway cattle. In the first year, he got no calves, probably because the bulls were too young. The next year, he got almost one hundred pregnant cows, but of these, he only got two live calves, and thirty of his cows died. Jones continued to experiment with cattalo for six years but had to sell his herd due to a recession in the 1890s. He did not, however, give up on the idea of raising cattalo for profit.[51] Either when Jones visited the Goodnight Ranch or when the two were at Yellowstone, he obviously discussed cattalo with Jimmy Owens and persuaded Owens to join him in a cattalo venture. The mystery is why did Owens decide to join Jones in his project? Owens had experience with some of the problems in raising cattalo while on the Goodnight ranch and undoubtedly asked Jones about

One of Mossom Boyd's cattalo, produced by crossing a buffalo bull with a domestic cow. Journal of Heredity, *1914*.

his problems with buffalo-cattle crosses in Garden City. Is it because Jones was a good salesman, or was Owens ready to move on from Yellowstone? Regardless, while the two were at Yellowstone, it appears they formulated a plan to start their own cattalo operation. The question was where could they get the land to start their enterprise? One possibility appeared to be in northern Arizona.

In 1891, Congress passed the Forest Reserve Act, withdrawing land from the public domain as "forest reserves" managed by the Department of the

Interior. One of the first areas to be so designated was the Grand Canyon Forest Reserve, which was established by President Benjamin Harrison in 1893. Forest reserves remained under the jurisdiction of the Department of the Interior until 1905, when Congress passed the Transfer Act, transferring their management to a new federal agency, the Bureau of Forestry, which later became the U.S. Forest Service.[52]

It appears that when Roosevelt visited Yellowstone in 1903, Jones spent some time with him talking about trying to save the buffalo, a cause Roosevelt supported. In early 1904, Jones contacted Roosevelt to get authorization to survey the Kaibab Plateau as a possible game preserve. This was the absenteeism mentioned by Major Pitcher in his letter to the secretary of interior about "Jones looking for a place for a cattalo operation."

In December 1904, Jones resigned as Yellowstone's gamekeeper and set out for Arizona to survey the proposed game preserve for the establishment of a buffalo herd, but he had an alternative motive for going. He wanted to look at the area for his and Owens's cattalo project. Jones contacted the son of U.S. forest supervisor Ernest Pratt to arrange his trip. In July 1905, he arrived in Kanab, Utah, where he met Edwin Wooley, a prominent Mormon rancher in the area, and Ernest Pratt.[53] The three toured the entire Kaibab Plateau and were overwhelmed by its beauty—the miles of unspoiled forest and the abundant wildlife. Everywhere they went, they saw deer, turkeys and the little white-tailed Kaibab squirrels. The entire area was so beautiful that Jones could not decide which area would be best for the game preserve, and he eventually recommended to Roosevelt that he make the entire Kaibab Plateau a game preserve, which he did.

While traveling, Jones entertained Wooley and Pratt with endless stories of his many adventures, fighting Indians, shooting buffalo and capturing musk ox in the far north. He also told them about his ideas of using the area to raise cattalo and explained their advantages over regular cattle. However, he apparently skipped over the problems involved in trying to breed buffalo and cattle. He was such a good salesman that by the time the three returned to Kanab he had convinced them to join him and his good friend Jimmy Owens in the cattalo venture. All that remained to be done was to get a permit to introduce buffalo to the Kaibab and raise money to purchase buffalo and cattle.[54]

When Jones returned, he gave Roosevelt such a glowing report of his trip to Arizona that it convinced the president of the Kaibab's value for wildlife and that he should establish the area as a game preserve and make it a place where a buffalo herd could be sustained. With Jones's urging,

Roosevelt designated most of the area north of the Grand Canyon as the Grand Canyon Game Preserve. Roosevelt stated that this designation "set the area up as a place for the protection of game animals and birds, and is to be recognized as a breeding place therefor."[55] However, predators were not protected because they killed the game animals, which were the ones Roosevelt and others of the time wanted to protect.

Jones's trip to the Kaibab couldn't have come at a better time. Not only did he persuade President Roosevelt to add lands to the Grand Canyon Forest Reserve, but he also obtained permission to fence a large portion of the southeast side of the Kaibab Plateau for his buffalo and cattle operation. He worked out an arrangement, undoubtedly with Roosevelt's help, where Washington, Jones and Owens would form a partnership. Jones and Owens would provide the buffalo and cattle, and the federal government would furnish the land, loan them a few buffalo and get a percentage of any profit made from the operation. This special arrangement was outlined in a letter from the secretary of agriculture to the secretary of interior, E.A. Hitchcock.

January 3rd, 1906
The Honorable E.A. Hitchcock
Secretary of the Interior,
Washington D.C.

Sir,

A special concession has been granted Col. Chas J. Jones in the Grand Canyon Forest Reservation in Arizona for the purpose of experimenting in the hybridizing of buffalo and cattle, the Government to retain a certain percentage of the produce. I am informed by Col. Jones that there are two buffalo bulls in the Yellowstone Park which the park authorities would be glad to have removed and which he could use to the advantage of the Government, and, himself, in the breeding of hybrids. If there is no objection to turning these two animals over to the jurisdiction of this Department, to be removed to the Grand Canyon Reserve, and loaned to Col. Jones, I recommend that it be done.

I have the honor to be Sir,
Very respectfully
Your obedient servant
James Wilson
Secretary of Agriculture[56]

Edwin Wooley, a prominent Kaibab rancher who invested in Owens and Jones's cattalo project. *Pipe Springs National Monument.*

On January 8, 1906, the agreement with the U.S. government was signed, and Owens and Jones had a place for their cattalo project, plus other long-term goals of introducing elk, moose, camels, zebras and Persian sheep, the latter of which they planned to cross with deer.[57] With enthusiasm high, it was time for Owens to move to Arizona to help Jones get the project started. Owens collected his last paycheck at Yellowstone on April 21, 1906.[58]

With the land secured, the next problem Owens and Jones faced was how to finance their project. Jones, being the promoter, already had Edwin Wooley and Ernest Pratt interested in the project. Others soon showed interest, and it wasn't long before not only Pratt and Wooley invested in the project but also local ranchers Benjamin Saunders and Frank Ascott, who had worked for Charles Goodnight on his ranch in Texas. In fact, Ascott became so enthused that he moved to the Kaibab to be closer to the project.[59]

In exchange for money needed to buy supplies and purchase access to water, each investor was given shares in an unofficial development company with Jones as president and Pratt as vice president. Others, like Wooley, provided some of their own cattle to be exchanged for Galloway cows that Jones thought best for breeding with buffalo because they were larger and could produce the buffalo-cattle cross without calving problems. However, he seemed to ignore the fact that Galloways were the same breed that he had problems with in his Garden City experiment and the research that showed that hybrid calves were actually smaller than either Galloway or buffalo calves.[60] With the cattle and money available, the partners were able to purchase one hundred Galloways, all the buffalo needed, and sixty-seven Persian sheep that Jones hoped to breed with deer to create a hearty wool-producing cross.

With the Galloway cattle purchased, the next chore was to acquire the buffalo. Since the 1880s, Jones had kept a buffalo herd near Garden City, Kansas. He used some of these animals for the Arizona herd, along with some from the Goodnight Ranch in Texas. Others he obtained from Señor E.J. Molera in Monterey, California, and a couple of bulls from Yellowstone that the park did not want. In June 1906, two carloads of buffalo arrived at Lund, Utah, the closest railhead to the Kaibab. The plan was for Owens,

Jones, Ascott and a forest ranger by the name of T.C. Hoyt to trail drive the herd 170 miles to their new home on the Kaibab Plateau. One carload of fifty-seven animals was in good shape, but the other herd of thirty was not. These were the animals from California, and to get to Lund, these animals had to be transported across Nevada in June, one of the hottest months of the summer. Being accustomed to the cool temperatures on the Monterey Peninsula, these animals suffered from the heat and arrived in Lund in very poor condition. Owens took one look at them and said, "These here critters are too dead beat to do anything but bury. They should have never left Monterey and they know it, and the quicker we sell them for steaks to the Mormons the better."[61] Jones, however, disagreed and wanted to try to drive them. The first day's effort soon demonstrated how difficult it was going to be to herd these eighty-seven buffalo to their new home on the Kaibab.[62]

The drive started early in the morning, with the Lund residents looking on. The idea was to put the bulls in the front, as the cows would follow. Unfortunately, as soon as the temperatures began to climb, the bulls refused to drive. They would lie down and would not get up, no matter how hard these experienced buffalo drivers tried to get them up and moving. At the end of the first day, they were only a mile from Lund, leaving 169 miles to go. It appeared that they were never going to get the herd to the Kaibab by driving them during the heat of the day. It was decided that instead they would try moving them at night when it was cooler and tempt the hungry animals with food. While the buffalo rested, Owens and Jones bought two wagons and filled them with sheaves of wheat. As the evening temperatures dropped, the herders got the bedded buffalo up, and by putting the wagons in front, they could periodically throw off a bundle of wheat to entice the animals to follow. Using this system, they slowly moved the herd to the Kaibab, with the exception of a few that died along the way.[63] Later, a second load of buffalo from Montana was shipped to Lund and added to the Kaibab herd. These animals were all in good condition, and when they were unloaded, Owens said, "They tore out across the desert and it was hours before we got them rounded up and headed south. We made thirty miles the first day."[64] Eventually, they got this second herd to the Kaibab and added them to the original herd grazing near Bright Angel Point on the North Rim. With the Galloway cattle and the buffalo now in place, the cattalo project could begin.

Shortly after the trip from Lund, the buffalo and the cattle were put together, but problems began to arise immediately. First, the buffalo began to leave the Kaibab Plateau to a more preferred area in House Rock Valley to the east, and the cattle had to be moved with them. Also, as found by other cattalo breeders, the buffalo and cattle were reluctant to breed with each other, so few offspring were produced. Of those cattle that were bred, about 25 percent produced a calf. If that calf was a heifer, the mother had a fifty-fifty chance of it being delivered alive. The chances of producing a male cattalo were even less. In most cases, if the calf was a male, it was aborted, and the cow died. On the rare occasion, if the male calf did live, it was sterile. Jones had encountered similar problems as early as 1887, when he had started cattalo experiments in Kansas and undoubtedly knew of Boyd's work, but it appears he neglected to tell his investors of the problems.[65] As a result, few cattalo were produced, no profit was returned to investors and the federal government saw no revenue from the project. By 1909, the project was deemed a failure, and the investors began to look for ways to recoup their losses.

One way to get their money back was by claiming the stock. Ascott took the cattle and Wooley the sheep. Owens, Wooley, Saunders and Jones kept the buffalo. In 1909, Jones quit the project and moved some of the buffalo to his ranch in New Mexico. In over twenty years of trying to raise cattalo, he had nothing to show but failure. Over time, a few animals were sold, like the dozen calves that were shipped to Chihuahua, where they became the nucleus for a buffalo herd along the border between New Mexico and the state of Chihuahua, Mexico. Owens eventually bought out Wooley and Saunders and became the sole owner of the twenty buffalo that remained. As the sole owner of the herd, Owens said he felt a great responsibility to care for them, even though he never saw any monetary reward. In the winter, he would graze his herd in House Rock Valley, a high desert area east of the Kaibab Plateau, and each spring, he would drive them to the Kaibab for the summer.[66] Except for moving his buffalo twice a year, Owens did little with the herd. Over time, his little buffalo herd multiplied. By 1922, it numbered almost one hundred animals, including a rare spotted cattalo steer that Owens named Old Spot. Each summer when Owens moved his buffalo herd to the top of the Kaibab Plateau, he took Old Spot, who became quite a tourist attraction. Buffalo Jones has always been given credit for bringing buffalo to Arizona, but Jimmy Owens was right there with him the entire time. Jones lost interest in Arizona buffalo after only three years and moved on to do other things. Owens, however, kept and cared for them on the North Rim for over twenty years. He is really the one that is responsible for buffalo being in Arizona today. He did all this while faithfully pursuing the job Teddy Roosevelt had hired him to do—hunt mountain lions.

SIX HUNDRED LIONS

They are there by hundreds," Roosevelt said, "and if they are not killed out they will ruin the deer life of that section, to say nothing of the cattle business in northern Arizona."[67] Mountain lions were the topic of conversation when Teddy Roosevelt met Owens in Yellowstone in 1903—or hunted with him in Wyoming in 1904. When Roosevelt visited the South Rim of the Grand Canyon in 1903, he met with some of his old San Juan Hill soldiers who had taken up residence in Arizona and Utah after the war. Knowing Roosevelt was a hunter, they obviously told him of the great number of deer north of the Grand Canyon and that mountain lions were preying on them. Roosevelt told Owens what he had heard about the Kaibab and insisted he go there and "exterminate lions."[68] Owens wanted to please the president, but he was currently employed as buffalo warden at Yellowstone. However, he did tell Roosevelt that he might be heading toward the Kaibab if Buffalo Jones found a suitable place for their cattalo ranch. Shortly thereafter, Jones, with some help from Roosevelt, did find a good place, and in 1906, Owens left Yellowstone to start raising cattalo in Arizona. This move put Owens in the right place at the right time to begin his twenty-plus years as a lion hunter.

During the late 1800s and early 1900s, a number of changes were occurring that would affect the North Rim and Jimmy Owens's life. In 1891, Congress passed the Forest Reserve Act, which gave the president authority to create forest reserves by executive order. President Benjamin Harrison was quick to take advantage of this act, and in 1893, he created

On his trip to the Grand Canyon in 1903, Roosevelt was told that "lions were killing all the deer on the North Rim." This information prompted him to hire Owens as Arizona's first forest guard in 1907. *National Park Service.*

the Grand Canyon Forest Reserve and put its management under the Department of Interior. On his 1903 visit to the South Rim of the Grand Canyon, Roosevelt, like everyone who sees the canyon for the first time, was so impressed with its grandeur that he made his famous statement: "Leave it as it is. You cannot improve on it. The ages have been at work on it, and man can only mar it. What you can do is to keep it for your children, your children's children, and for all who come after you, as the one great sight which every American should see."[69]

In 1905, a new federal agency was created, the Bureau of Forestry, which later became the United States Forest Service under the Department of Agriculture. Since this new agency's responsibility was directed more toward the management of the forest resources, such as grazing and timber, than the Department of Interior, management responsibility of the Grand Canyon Forest Reserve was transferred to it when Congress passed the Transfer Act in 1905.

Following his trip to the Grand Canyon in 1903, Roosevelt, who was concerned about the declining numbers of wildlife, started creating game reserves by executive order. One of the first was to merge the Grand Canyon Forest Preserve into the 612,000-acre Grand Canyon National Game Reserve in 1906. This newly created game reserve was established "for the protection of game animals and as a breeding place therefor."[70] Roosevelt also showed the thinking of the time when he said, "The preservation of game and of wildlife, generally aside from the noxious species, on these reserves is of incalculable benefit to the people as a whole."[71] In other words, what he was saying was that there were "good" species, such as deer, and there were "bad" species, such as mountain lions, that preyed on the good species and, therefore, needed to be eliminated.

To deal with the predator situation, one of the first things each game reserve required was someone to make sure game was protected. Such individuals were known as forest guards and were paid seventy-five to ninety dollars a month, from which they had to buy uniforms and supply at least three horses.[72] The forest guard's job was to protect the desirable species, not only from poachers but also from predators, such as wolves, coyotes and lions. Roosevelt needed a forest guard for his recently created Grand Canyon Game Preserve, and as fate would have it, who was already in the area but his acquaintance Jimmy Owens. Roosevelt quickly contacted Owens to see if he would take the job and, in 1907, appointed Owens as the preserve's first forest guard. This appointment also made Owens Arizona's first game warden. Owens remained in this position until 1919, when Grand Canyon National Park was created.

Since hunting was not allowed on game preserves, most forest guards primarily protected wildlife from poaching. Owens's job, though, was a little different, due to his skill as a hunter. His duties were to shoot, trap or by any other means remove predators, primarily mountain lions. In this regard, the forest service also allowed him to guide hunting parties at his own discretion, as long as it resulted in the taking of predators. Owens was also allowed to collect bounties ranging from $15 to $100 for each lion taken. Because he was a predator hunter, many people thought he worked for the Predator and Rodent Control branch of the U.S. Department of Agriculture, which employed a number of hunters and trappers. This was not the case. Except for a couple of months with the Predator and Rodent Control Agency, Owens always worked for the United States Forest Service, until he went into his own business of guiding lion hunts.

On getting the forest guard position, Owens's first job was to train a pack of dogs for hunting. This training involved teaching his dogs to trail only lions and to not chase animals such as deer and coyotes. Since he

Above: Owens's first job on arriving on the Kaibab was to start training a pack of hounds. *Grand Canyon National Park Museum Collection, no. 05301.*

Opposite: Uncle Jimmy with Pot Hound, whose collar claimed that the hound had been in on the kill of 450 lions. *Rex Beach*, Oh Shoot!: Confessions of an Agitated Sportsman, *1921.*

had already been in the area for a year getting his cattalo project going with Buffalo Jones, he had become well acquainted with ranchers and other houndsmen in the area. Most likely, he purchased a few trained dogs to get his pack started, but as time went on, he raised his own dogs, which were crosses from English and southern black and tan bloodhounds.[73] His dogs had a variety of colorful names, such as Fanny, Daniel Boone and Tub, but two were special, Ranger and Pot. Ranger, one of his first dogs, was a big black and tan dog he called Forest Ranger, or Ranger for short. Ranger was a large dog and was said to have a voice that could be "heard for miles."[74] As Ranger got older, he was subsequently replaced by another dog, who became a legend on the Kaibab, Pot Hound, or Pot, as he was better known. Pot wore a collar with an engraved plate attached, reading, "I Have Been at the Killing of More Than 450 Lions."[75]

Pot had a hard start in life. One of Owens's better dogs was Fanny. She hunted with the other hounds every day, including a hunt when she was quite pregnant. The hunt turned out to be long and exhausting, and afterward, Fanny became sick. Jim tried to doctor her as best as he could in his remote camp, but Fanny got no better. Finally, she gave birth to several puppies, but all were born dead except for one white and tan pup. Shortly after giving birth, Fanny died without ever producing milk to feed the newborn pup. Owens kept the puppy alive as best as he could by feeding him canned milk with an eyedropper. At first, he fed him with warm diluted milk, but later, he was able to switch him over to a bottle. At night, Owens would put the little white and tan pup in an old woolen sock and put him inside his warm cabin. As Pot got a little older, he still wore the woolen sock, but when Owens was moving camp, Pot was carried in a bag attached to his saddle horn.

Pot, who was destined to be a lion hound, also experienced lions at an early age. Owens brought a lion kitten to camp when Pot was only a few weeks old. The two became instant friends. They would eat together out of the same dish, and as they both got older, they would play together. In spite of his rough start, and because of having been fed special food, Pot thrived and developed such a love for food that the name Pot Hound was a natural for him. As he got older, Pot was trained to trail lions under one of Owens's favorite dogs, Ranger. He was a little smaller than Ranger but developed the same deep voice, and it wasn't long before he became the pack leader when Ranger grew too old to hunt. Because of the attention Pot had been given, he and Owens formed a special relationship. Pot was the only dog that was given the run of camp, and Owens would talk to him like he was another person. It was a special bond between man and dog.

Pot lived to be thirteen or fourteen years old and died doing what he loved, hunting lions. Uncle Jim had been hunting in some rough country on the west side of the plateau and lost track of his dogs. Losing them was not an uncommon occurrence because in the rough country they would often get out of hearing range. Owens didn't worry about it because when the dogs finally got tired, they would come back to his camp. However, this time, Pot didn't return with the other hounds. Owens set out to look for him and eventually found where he had slipped off an icy cliff and fell to his death near Big Springs Ranger Station. No other hound ever took the place of or received the affection from Uncle Jim as Pot Hound.[76]

As was the case with most houndsmen, Owens's dogs came first. They were the tools of his trade, and at the end of the day, his dogs received first consideration, then came his horses and finally himself.[77] Since there was no canned dog food available, Owens fed his dogs horse meat acquired from wild horses in the area. Like all houndsmen, he also fed them a little lion meat to reward them for catching a lion. Even though there were plenty of deer, he wasn't allowed to kill one, since he was there to protect them. A good example of how well Owens treated his dogs was an incident related by Dan Judd of Fredonia. Judd was a forest ranger on the Kaibab and happened upon Owens's camp shortly after he had guided President Roosevelt in 1913. As a thank-you for the hunt, Roosevelt had sent Jim a small balloon-silk tent, which was waterproof and made such a light bundle that it could be carried on the back of his saddle. According to Judd, shortly after receiving the tent, Uncle Jim was caught away from camp in a heavy rainstorm. To avoid getting wet, he lay under an old tarpaulin for shelter while his five hounds were sleeping snugly in the silk tent.[78]

When Owens would go on a hunt, he would pack supplies for two or three weeks, and when possible, a forest ranger would be assigned to accompany him because of the risk of an accident. In many cases, though, this was not possible, and most of the time, Uncle Jim would be by himself.[79] On one particular trip, he was gone for eleven months without seeing another soul.[80] On another, he and his nephew Ed Cox were snowbound for three weeks by five feet of snow. They waited for the weather to warm so that

Uncle Jim Owen   July 1919

Left: Uncle Jimmy took good care of his hounds, like sewing up an injured foot on one of his dogs. *Grand Canyon National Park Museum Collection, no. 05285.*

Below: Owens often packed hunting camps into the more remote portions of the Kaibab Plateau. *Grand Canyon National Park Museum Collection, no. 05290.*

they could get out, but it just kept snowing. Finally, after their horses and dogs had gone four days without food, they decided to get out as best as they could. The only way they could travel was to take turns walking ahead of the horses and dogs and tramp down the snow. Each man would tramp out a trail for about ten minutes before they tired and had to be relieved. Fortunately, after they had covered about four excruciating miles, they met a group of friends who had become concerned about them being gone so long and had set out to find them.[81]

Hunting lions near the Grand Canyon had its risks, as a lion would often go over the rim to get away from the dogs, thus creating a dangerous situation for both dog and man. One such incident was described by Bill

Uncle Jimmy hunted year-round and often camped in the snow. *Kaibab National Forest, no. F223867.*

Mace, a forest ranger assigned to accompany Owens on a hunt. Uncle Jim and Mace were out with the hounds near the canyon rim on the west side of the Kaibab. As they rode along the rim, Jim pointed out the place where he had met a full-grown lion almost face to face, and he couldn't do much about it. He recalled that he had had a long chase one day, which ended when the cougar went down through the cliffs into the canyon in the late afternoon. The next morning, Owens prepared a small parcel of food and followed the hounds on foot down through a break in the canyon wall. The hounds eventually picked up the trail of the cat, but it led them on a merry chase by winding up and down, over and back, through heavy underbrush and along boulder-strewn slopes. This chase continued until both dogs and master were about exhausted, before they finally made the capture. It had been a warm day, and since he had discovered a small spring, Uncle Jim decided to give the hounds a cougar steak and spend the night there.

It took most of the next day to make the climb out of the canyon, and as he neared the summit, he spotted a break in the cliff where he figured he could get through. The hounds were left to find their own way back, while Uncle Jim began the climb up the cliff. When almost to the top, and about worn out, he reached a place where, as he expressed it, he "was just hanging by teeth and toenails" on a narrow ledge with a direct drop of about seventy-five feet. As he struggled to keep from falling, he looked up to find a big cougar staring at him, with only a few feet between them. As it took both hands to maintain his hold, there was no chance to use his .45 pistol. He and the lion just stared at each other, waiting to see who was going to give way first. Fortunately, before Jim lost his grip on the rocks, the lion turned and retreated back up the cliff. Owens completed his climb, and when he reached the top of the rim, he searched the locality, without success. The lion had left no tracks on the bare rock, and the dogs were too tired to try to trail it.[82]

Owens was not always so lucky. One morning while running after a lion he fell and injured his back. He was unable to move for hours, but finally got to his hands and knees and crawled two miles to his camp. Fortunately, he had made his camp under a tree, so by holding on to branches, he could manage to get up and down. He lived this way for a week while recuperating.[83]

Buffalo Jones, who occasionally hunted with Owens, with two of Owens's hounds, Sounder and Ranger. *Zane Grey,* Tales of Lonely Trails.

Besides forest rangers accompanying Owens, Buffalo Jones also took part in some of his hunts. Jones, however, was quick to realize that there was more money to be made from a live lion than a dead one. There was a demand from zoos and private individuals for live mountain lions, so he and Owens began to capture and keep some cats alive rather than kill them. To accomplish this feat took some skill and daring. First, the dogs had to tree a lion. Next, Jones, who loved the challenge, would hook a lasso to a pole and climb the tree until he could reach the lion. He would then attempt to put the rope around the animal's neck. Once that was accomplished, the lion would be pulled out of the tree, and Owens would to get another rope around the lion's hind legs. Once on the ground, the two men would tie all four feet together, clip the lion's nails and muzzle it so it would not hurt man, dog or the pack horse that had to carry it. These lions were then shipped around the world.[84]

Owens continued to hunt lions virtually every day, in summer and in winter, mostly by himself, until 1915, when things began to change. In 1915, the Biological Survey's Predator and Rodent Control Branch of the U.S Department of Agriculture took over predator control from the Forest Service. This meant that for the first time, people other than Owens were taking predators, although most of the Biological Survey's work on the North Rim was focused on wolves and coyotes. Jim, however, continued to work for the Forest Service until 1919, when he resigned to focus his entire efforts on guided hunts. He did this for an additional four years, until 1922, when, due to age-related hearing loss, he could no longer follow his hounds.[85] Many people thought Owens worked for the Predator and Rodent Control branch of the Biological Survey, but in reality, his time employed in government service was with the Forest Service. The only work he did for Predator and Rodent Control was for fifteen days in 1919.[86]

During his tenure on the Kaibab, Owens undoubtedly did more to virtually eliminate lions than any other person, but just how many he took is debatable. Estimates of his kill range from 500 to 600 lions over the twenty-two-year period that he hunted, with one estimate going as high as 1,165.[87] The 500 to 600 number appears to have originated from a comment made by A.A. Nichol, a biologist at the University of Arizona. In a report on the Kaibab, he stated that 600 lions were killed by Owens, but gave no information on where he got that number. Since then, this number has been repeated by other authors and seems to have become the accepted number. However, this large number of cats must certainly be questioned because other evidence suggests the total might have been somewhat lower.

In 1921, Joseph Dixon from the University of California attempted to get an accurate count of the number of lions killed on the Kaibab. To do so, he first contacted W.C. Henderson, who was acting bureau chief for the Biological Survey, which was the primary agency in charge of predator control on the Kaibab. He soon found that Henderson could not provide any reliable numbers, since most of his hunters only took a few lions in connection with their other hunting operations against coyotes, bobcats and wolves. Since Henderson was of little help in providing any information on lion kills, Dixon then contacted the Biological Survey inspectors in the region. These inspectors had closer contact with various predator control agents than Henderson and provided more definite, but not necessarily more accurate, numbers.[88] One such inspector who Dixon relied heavily on was George Holman. Holman was a government scientist working for the Cooperative Campaign for the Destruction of Predatory Animals in Utah, which was a joint effort of the Biological Survey and the Utah State Livestock Board.[89] Holman knew that Owens had taken most of the lions killed on the Kaibab but thought the numbers had been exaggerated.[90]

Holman's reason for doubt was that some of the lions killed by Owens were taken on guided hunts with high-profile personalities, such as Zane Grey and Teddy Roosevelt. As part of these hunts, Owens would talk about his past experiences and accomplishments, and both Grey and Roosevelt wrote about his exploits.[91] As time went on, more and more people wanted to hear about the excitement of his hunts, and Owens was always glad to tell his stories. Holman thought that this repeated telling of hunting stories had inflated the actual number of lions killed, and because of this, the numbers were untrustworthy.[92] Holman then looked to the Forest Service for more accurate numbers, since it was Owens's employer. Like the Biological Survey, the Forest Service records were sketchy, but Holman was able to find that Owens had actually reported that he had killed sixty-seven lions in a five-year period.[93] Using these figures, Holman then calculated that Owens probably took about two hundred lions during his time on the Kaibab.

Based on more recent data, the two hundred number seems more reasonable. According to figures compiled by noted wildlife biologist Aldo Leopold in the 1920s, the number of deer that the Kaibab could support, without overgrazing the range, was between twenty and thirty thousand animals.[94] Such a deer herd would support the highest number of lions possible, since prey regulates predator numbers. During the late 1970s and early 1980s, the Arizona Game and Fish Department conducted an extensive mountain lion study on the Kaibab. At that time, it was estimated that the Kaibab deer population was about twenty thousand animals, similar to the population estimated by Leopold.[95] The results of the Game and Fish study revealed that approximately forty to fifty lions existed on the Kaibab in the absence of any type of predator control.[96] This number of lions would be similar to what Owens would have had to hunt when he first arrived in the area. Even though lion numbers might have increased due to lions moving into the area as the deer population skyrocketed out of control, there still is no way he could have taken six hundred lions in twenty-two years. Holman's number of two hundred is much more realistic and was supported by the Arizona Game and Fish study.

The 200 number also seems to be substantiated by Pot Hound, even though he wore a collar that stated, "I Have been at the Killing of More than 450 Lions." Pot was undoubtedly a good dog, but not that good. If you look at the average life expectancy of a hunting hound, they probably cannot hunt more than ten to twelve years. If that was the case with Pot, and he was able to hunt until he was twelve, he would have been at the killings of about 40 lions a year. Owens's kills, reported to the Forest Service over a five-year period was 67, or about 13 lions per year—far short of the 450 accredited to Pot.

There are, however, two possibilities that could have increased the number Owens took. One was taking lions away from the Kaibab. Mountain lions occur throughout southern Utah, and certainly, Owens would travel there to hunt. He probably did not spend a lot of time in other areas, however, as he was hired to specifically hunt the North Rim country. The second thing that could increase the number is what a person considers to be a mountain lion kill. Most people would visualize a kill as the death of a cat capable of moving around on its own. This, however, was not always the case. As early as domestic livestock entered the western ranges, ranchers began to pay a hunter ten or twenty dollars to take lions that were killing their cattle or sheep. To help the ranching community, state and county governments also started paying bounties on predatory animals. Where some people looked at a lion as a walking breathing animal, others looked at them as anything that could be identified as a lion, namely fetuses. Taking advantage of the bounty system, predator hunters bountied not only a female lion but also all of her unborn young. The Forest Service allowed Owens to collect bounties for the lions he took, but whether he bountied fetuses is not known, though his partner, Buffalo Jones, certainly did. Records show that Jones killed a mother mountain lion with nine unborn kittens and collected ten bounty payments from Coconino County.[97] If Owens did take advantage of the bounty system in this way, then the total number he took could be much higher than the two hundred. The number of lions Owens actually took will never be known, but by 1930, they were considered rare on the North Rim.[98] They were rare enough that Owens's success affected the Kaibab deer herd long after his death.

ONE HUNDRED THOUSAND DEER

When Uncle Jimmy Owens first arrived on the North Rim, he found the area overrun with livestock. At the time, it was estimated that there were over two hundred thousand sheep, twenty thousand cattle and approximately two thousand horses and, of course, the hundred or so buffalo that he and Buffalo Jones had introduced.[99] The high number of livestock allowed was the result of a weakness in the Forest Reserve Act. When the act was passed in 1891, its objective was to protect timber and water. The reserves were not closed to mining, and little attention was given to regulating or reducing livestock numbers.[100] Another thing the Forest Reserve Act failed to protect was wildlife. In addition to all of the livestock, it was estimated that about four thousand mule deer used the area.[101] There were no restrictions on killing deer for local settlers or the Paiute Indians that inhabited the area. This lack of wildlife protection concerned Roosevelt and was instrumental in his creating game preserves and hiring people like Owens as forest guards to protect wildlife.

As Roosevelt looked around, he felt that if something was not done some species of animals might be totally eliminated. The buffalo, for instance, had virtually disappeared from the prairies. Birds with beautiful plumed feathers, such as those from terns, ibis and roseate spoonbills, which adorned ladies' hats, had been decimated.[102] Others, like the heath hen and passenger pigeon, were all but extinct. Protecting animals from poaching and market hunting was one way to protect wildlife, but like many other individuals of his time, Roosevelt thought that if wildlife populations were to return to

By the mid-1920s, deer numbers on the Kaibab Plateau were estimated to be as high as fifty to one hundred thousand. *National Park Service.*

their former numbers, predators also had to be controlled. Thus, the "war on predators" began.

Of all the preserves, the Grand Canyon Game Preserve was of special interest to Roosevelt. The Kaibab Plateau deer population was noted for its large bucks with exceptional antlers that were coveted by hunters. Roosevelt, being a hunter himself, recognized the outstanding quality of these deer. He wanted to protect them, not only from poachers and market hunters but also predators. The latter was why he hired Uncle Jimmy Owens. From his experience in meeting Owens, Roosevelt knew he was the man for the job. Owens was an experienced outdoorsman of the West, which Roosevelt admired. He also had the lion hunting skills to put into action one of Roosevelt's game management principles: "If you wanted more game you had to get rid of predators." This simple premise was the thinking of the time, but its implementation created a crisis on the Kaibab that would far outlive both Roosevelt and Owens.

As Owens surveyed the North Rim as a new employee of the newly created Forest Service, he couldn't help but notice the deplorable condition of the range due to all of the livestock grazing in the late 1800s. By the time he arrived, however, the Forest Service had started to try to reduce the number of livestock on the Grand Canyon Game Preserve. Even though it had made significant progress in reducing livestock numbers, there were still twenty thousand sheep, nine thousand cattle and an unrecorded number of horses grazing on the Kaibab Plateau.[103] Deer numbers at the same time were estimated at between three thousand and four thousand.[104] The increase in forage due to the reduction in livestock grazing and the elimination of hunting undoubtedly benefited deer, but people thought that if you were really going to have more deer, you had to get rid of the animals that preyed on them, namely mountain lions, wolves, coyotes and bobcats.

Jimmy Owens's job was primarily to kill lions, while trappers working for the Biological Survey took coyotes, wolves, bobcats and even golden eagles. As the predators were removed, the deer herd began to increase, and by 1918, it was estimated that fifteen thousand deer inhabited the Kaibab Plateau.[105] To most people, this success was attributed to Owens because he was taking the primary deer predator, one that was capable of killing as many as fifty deer a year. Removing predators like the mountain lion appeared to be a huge factor in building a deer population, but as the killing of predators continued, it became obvious that it might be too successful.

As the years went by, deer numbers kept increasing to levels never seen before, reaching an estimated high of one hundred thousand in 1924.[106] This huge deer herd, plus over eight thousand head of livestock that still remained on the range, soon wiped out the small gains that had been made in range improvement. Virtually all vegetation within reach of a deer standing on its hind feet was eaten on both the summer and winter range, and thousands of deer died of starvation each winter.[107] The range situation became so bad that in 1924, Secretary of Agriculture Henry C. Wallace appointed a committee of leading conservationists to look into the Kaibab deer situation.

This Kaibab Investigation Committee, as it was called, consisted of representatives from both governmental and various stakeholders, such as the Boone and Crocket Club, Audubon Society, National Park Service, Livestock Breeders Association and American Game Protective Association. When this committee met on the North Rim, it was also joined by local representatives of the Forest Service, Biological Survey and Geological Survey. At Wallace's direction, this group was to examine the range, determine the number of deer on the Kaibab, and make recommendations on how to reduce their numbers.[108]

On August 17, 1924, this committee met at Big Springs Ranger Station and set out to examine the range. What the members found was deplorable. On the summer range, shrubs were virtually eliminated, and even trees like aspen, pine and fir had been eaten off as high as a man's head. The large parks, like VT Park, were being turned into dust bowls. Conditions on the winter range were even worse. Forage that would normally be used by deer in the winter months was already being eaten by deer in the summer, leaving little for those animals that would move off the plateau in the fall. Prior to the Investigation Committee's survey, a figure of twenty thousand deer had been estimated by the Biological Survey in 1923. After the survey, members of the committee believed that the deer herd far exceeded this number. All agreed that the Kaibab deer herd numbered at least fifty thousand, with

By the late 1920s, vegetation on the summer range was severely impacted by too many deer. *Kaibab National Forest.*

some estimates going as high as one hundred thousand deer. It was apparent that if something was not, done a "deer disaster" was about to happen.[109]

Based on its observations of the deer range, the committee made several recommendations aimed at "preserving the Kaibab deer herd for all time with the maximum number of deer that the area will support."[110] First, it was recommended that all livestock not owned by local ranchers be removed and that grazing numbers be reduced. Second, the committee suggested that the deer herd be cut in half.[111] To accomplish this goal, the committee suggested three courses of action. First, capture deer alive and move them to other locations. Second, allow sport hunting, which had not been allowed since 1906, when the Grand Canyon Game Preserve was created. If enough deer were not removed by these two means, then professional hunters and Forest Service employees would shoot deer.[112] It is interesting to note that at the time efforts were being made to reduce the number of deer, no restrictions were put on the taking of predators that would kill deer, primarily mountain lions. Owens just continued to hunt and kill lions.

By the late 1920s, winter range vegetation was eaten off as high as a deer could reach. *Kaibab National Forest.*

The Forest Service, which administered the Grand Canyon Game Preserve, acted as quickly as it could to implement the committee's recommendations. Grazing quotas were reduced. Traps were built around water holes to capture deer, which were then offered for sale at a cost of thirty-five dollars each. The traps, however, did little to reduce deer numbers, because few deer were captured and even fewer people wanted to buy them. When it was obvious that trapping would not remove enough deer, the Forest Service asked the State of Arizona to authorize a hunting season—the first since 1906, when the Grand Canyon Game Preserve was established. In October 1924, for a fee of five dollars, a hunter could take 3 deer of either sex. The problem was getting hunters to the Kaibab. Roads were poor, and the trip was difficult. Only 270 hunters managed the trip, and they took only 675 deer. The next year, hunters were allowed to take only 1 deer. Again, few people were able to make the long trip to the Kaibab, and only 392 deer were taken, 40 of which had to be condemned because of their poor physical condition, which demonstrated the poor conditions of the deer herd.[113] Similar hunts occurred in 1926 and 1927, but in 1928, problems arose. Even though there was a hunt each year, the annual kill was less than 1,000 deer.[114] The Forest

Government hunters hired by the U.S. Forest Service with a truckload of deer they had shot in an effort to reduce deer numbers on the Kaibab Plateau. *U.S. Forest Service.*

Service, acting out of desperation, felt that this was not going to reduce the deer herd. More deer needed to be removed, so in 1928, even though there was a sport hunt, the Forest Service decided to employ professional hunters to kill deer. Shooting began on December 14, 1928. Hunters traveled on horseback looking for deer. When they killed a deer, they had to field dress it themselves, get it to a place where it could be loaded in a wagon or truck and hauled to a base camp for further processing. Using this method, hunters took 1,124 deer.[115]

Almost before it started, the killing of deer by professional hunters caused controversy. The Arizona Game and Fish Department, known as the Department of Conservation in 1924, was responsible for the management of wildlife in Arizona. This agency felt that this also included wildlife on Forest Service lands, since wildlife belonged to the people of the state. Arizona thought that if deer had to be killed on the Kaibab, it should be done by sport hunters, not professional hunters. This jurisdictional battle between the federal government and the State of Arizona became so bad that Arizona governor Hunt threatened to call in the National Guard to stop the killing. The ensuing battle between the two agencies finally went to the Supreme Court, which ruled that the secretary of agriculture had the right to kill deer to protect the Kaibab's vegetation.[116] A year later, however, the Forest Service gave up using paid hunters, and an agreement between the federal government and the State of Arizona was worked out, allowing the state to establish a hunting season. Ever since, the state, through the Arizona Game and Fish Department, has managed the sport hunting of the Kaibab deer herd.[117]

Unfortunately, the committee's recommendations were not implemented quickly enough. Due to the poor condition of the range, deer began to starve and die. Dead deer were found everywhere on the Kaibab Plateau, and it was estimated that 75 percent of the fawns born in the summer died over the winter. Additional die-offs occurred in 1926, 1927 and 1928, reducing the deer herd to an estimated thirty thousand animals.[118] Periodic die-offs and deplorable range conditions continued to exist into the 1930s, but Owens would not experience them. He left the North Rim around 1929.

During the time that various attempts were made to reduce deer numbers, a rather unique suggestion on how to accomplish a reduction was offered by Jimmy Owens's friend Zane Grey. Rather than shoot deer, why not just have cowboys drive them across the Grand Canyon to the South Rim, where the range was in much better condition. There were men in the area, including Owens, who were used to working with wild livestock, and Grey thought deer should be no problem for them to handle. To most people, Grey's idea of driving deer seemed ridiculous. Anyone who has been around wildlife knows you can't drive wild animals to places they don't want to go. Nevertheless, Grey somehow convinced George McCormick of Flagstaff of the idea. McCormick, who was a cattle rancher, liked the idea and suggested to the State of Arizona that he could organize a deer drive to herd thousands of deer off the North Rim, into the Grand Canyon and up to the South Rim. Governor Hunt also liked the plan and lobbied the Forest Service to support the idea. The Forest Service, desperate for a solution to the deer problem, signed on. At a price of $2.50 per animal, McCormick contracted to drive five to ten thousand deer across the canyon.[119] Zane Grey, who was already a famous author, was also connected with a Hollywood movie company, Lasky Studios, later known as Paramount Pictures. It offered McCormick $5,000 for the rights to film the drive. People in Flagstaff also raised another $1,000 if McCormick could drive some deer as far south as Flagstaff.[120]

On December 16, 1924, fifty cowboys and seventy Navajo men started the Great Deer Drive to try to push deer across the Grand Canyon.[121] Since Owens was in the area, knew the country, and the drive was to start in House Rock Valley where his buffalo wintered, there is a good chance he was involved. As one can imagine, trying to drive wild deer, not to mention across the Grand Canyon, proved to be one of the biggest fiascos in the history of wildlife management, but it was also one of the most publicized, because Grey described it in detail in his book *The Deer Stalker*. In the selection of characters for his book, Grey used Jimmy Owens as the character Jim Evans, the local mountain lion hunter.[122]

To execute the drive, the riders formed a line around a large portion of the eastern winter range and started to drive deer toward a trail that led into the vastness of the Grand Canyon. Near the pass where the trail began, several men, along with Grey's photographer, were stationed where they could count the deer as they were driven by. The drive started out well, with the drivers moving hundreds of deer toward the canyon. However, as they got closer to the pass, deer started to run back through the line of drivers, and by the time the drive was completed, not a single deer was driven into the canyon, and not a single foot of film was shot.[123] Deer were just not going to be driven where they did not want to go. For his efforts, McCormick didn't make a dime, and the only people to receive any money for their efforts were the Navajo drivers, who demanded McCormick pay them two dollars per day in advance. Kaibab District forest ranger R.H. Rutledge summed up the entire attempted drive by saying that it was "the most interesting failure I have ever witnessed."[124]

Although the removal of lions by Owens is often pointed out as the main reason for the tremendous increase and subsequent die-off of deer on the Kaibab, Owens's lion removal was just one of many factors that caused the deer population irruption and subsequent die-off. The range was tremendously overstocked with both sheep and cattle, and government trappers employed by the Biological Survey also took predators, such as coyotes, bobcats and a few wolves, at the same time. With deer numbers near 100,000, the range was severely overpopulated. Beginning in the winter of 1925–26 and continuing into the 1930s, thousands of deer died due to starvation, reducing the herd to an estimated 14,000 animals by 1932. Since that time, deer numbers have fluctuated due to various levels of hunter harvest, which took both male and female animals, plus severe drought and catastrophic forest fires that reduced available forage. In 2020, the deer population was estimated at between 10,000 and 15,000 animals.[125] Owens certainly cannot be blamed for everything that happened between deer and mountain lions on the North Rim. He was simply doing the job President Roosevelt asked him to do.

GUIDE FOR THE RICH
AND FAMOUS

I n 1907, Buffalo Jones was on a lecture tour throughout the eastern
United States, showing pictures of how he and Jimmy Owens were
capturing mountain lions on the North Rim of the Grand Canyon.
One of the lectures' attendees was a young dentist by the name of Zane
Grey. Grey was bored with his dental business and had started trying to do
some writing but was having little success. Always interested in the outdoors,
Grey thought it might be interesting to attend Jones's lecture. Jones, in his
flamboyant way, talked about riding horseback through the magnificent pine
country of the North Rim and roping and capturing lions on the edge of
the beautiful Grand Canyon. Jones's descriptions and pictures excited Grey,
and he thought such an adventure might make a good book, so he arranged
a hunting trip with Jones and Owens for 1908. Prior to this time, Owens
had done little guiding, even though the Forest Service did not restrict him
from doing so. As long as he was killing lions, it was happy. A few locals
occasionally went with him, but the remoteness of the North Rim made him
virtually unknown anywhere else, until Zane Grey wrote about his hunt in
Roping Lions in the Grand Canyon.[126]

When Grey arrived at Owens's camp for his hunt in 1908, he found it
to be a crude log cabin with a large stone fireplace. Inside were a table
and chairs, a bed and a well-stocked cupboard. On the outside were deer
antlers; coyote, bobcat and lion skins; and lion claws nailed everywhere.[127]
Shortly after arriving, Grey learned that Owens and Jones were going to
try to capture some lions alive to send to various zoos.[128] The technique

they planned to use was to trail a lion with hounds until it climbed a tree. One person would then climb the tree or use a long pole with a rope noose attached and try to get a noose around the animal's neck. In some instances, the lion might get over a limb and would remain dangling in the air until it passed out. In this case, a stick would be tied in its mouth so it couldn't bite anyone, "hogtied," and a collar put around its neck. In other situations, the lion might jump to the ground rather than stay in the tree. When this happened, the person who had the rope around the lion's neck would tie his end to a tree and the other person would try to get a rope on the animal's hind legs. The lion would then be "stretched out" until it started to lose consciousness due to the rope around its neck. The lion could then be tied down, placed on a pack saddle and packed back to camp, where it was chained to a tree until it could be

Zane Grey, who hunted with Owens in 1908, used him as a character in his book *Roping Lions in the Grand Canyon*. *Wikisource,* Tales of Lonely Trails, *by Zane Grey.*

shipped to its final destination.[129] Obviously, some danger existed in getting the lion subdued, and in several instances, Owens was mauled and scratched while attempting to take a lion alive.[130] During Grey's two-week hunt, ten lions were captured and shipped to zoos around the country. Most of the cats were taken north, where there was access to roads and railways, but in some instances, lions were put in cages atop a pack horse and packed across the canyon to El Tovar Lodge. There, they could be put on the railroad and shipped to destinations farther south.[131] Thanks to Jones's exciting talks and Grey's sensationalized book, people began to learn about Uncle Jimmy and started to contact him about guided hunts.

To hunt with Owens, one had to be hardy, as getting to the North Rim in the early 1900s was not an easy chore. There were two routes, one long and one short. The long route left Flagstaff, Arizona, and traveled across the Navajo Indian Reservation to Lee's Ferry, which was the only place to cross the Colorado River for hundreds of miles. Lee's Ferry itself could be quite an adventure, since it was nothing more than a small flat-bottomed barge pulled by cable across the river. Without today's Glen Canyon Dam to regulate water flow, the river could be dangerously high at times, making the crossing extremely risky. After crossing the river, one then had to travel along the foot of the Vermillion Cliffs and onto the Kaibab Plateau. This 160-mile route was a hot, dry trip, especially across the Navajo lands. The shorter route also left from Flagstaff but went directly to the South Rim of

During the summer months, Owens usually hunted from his cabin in Harvey Meadow. *Grand Canyon National Park Museum Collection, no. 05276.*

Live-captured lions were packed back to Owens's camp and chained to a tree until they could be shipped to their final destination. *Grand Canyon National Park Museum Collection, no. 05551.*

When Roosevelt hunted with Owens in 1913, he crossed the Colorado River on David Rust's tram, as these people are doing. He described the crossing as a "bully good ride." *Grand Canyon National Park Museum Collection, no. 05435.*

the canyon. From there, one descended by horseback into the canyon via the Bright Angel Trail and crossed the river on Rust's tramway. This tram, built by David Rust, consisted of a cable stretched above the river. Attached to this cable was a metal cage. To cross, one got into the cage and pulled it across to the other side.[132] Once across, a person could then ascend to the North Rim via a trail up Bright Angel Creek, topping out near Owens's cabin in Harvey Meadow. However, if the snow was deep on the North Rim or Bright Angel Creek was flooding, the traveler was forced to take the longer route through Lee's Ferry or use the older Bass Trail.

Before Rust built a trail and constructed a tram to cross the canyon, an earlier crossing was constructed by William Bass in the late 1890s. Bass, who arrived at the Grand Canyon in 1884, had several mining claims on both sides of the river. To get to these claims, he constructed a rough and steep trail across the canyon, but the big obstacle was getting across the river. To accomplish this, Bass built a tramway consisting of a 450-foot cable stretched 50 feet above the river. Attached to this cable was a rickety wooden cage with a gate on both ends. The cage could then be pulled across from one side to the other. In this way, it allowed one to get across the river, along with horses and supplies.[133]

An example of how difficult this crossing was is exemplified by the experienced filmmakers Rex Beach and Fred Stone, plus several camera men, when they went to hunt with Owens. Beach and Stone, like Zane Grey, had attended one of Buffalo Jones's lectures, where they were fascinated by his pictures of roping mountain lions. To them, it looked dangerous, but Jones assured them it was not a risk because mountain lions were shy animals. After listening to Jones, they thought a trip to hunt and rope lions might be an adventure. Not knowing how to go about setting up such a hunt, they contacted Ambrose Means, who worked with Jimmy Owens from time to time. Means told them that he could take them to the North Rim for a hunt with Owens.

When Beach's party met Means on the South Rim in the spring of 1914, the plan was to take the Bright Angel Trail and Rust's tram across the canyon. As the group stood in front of the El Tovar Hotel, Means informed them that plans had changed. Due to rain and melting snow, Bright Angel Creek was running high and was impassible. Instead, they would have to go twenty-five miles to the west to take the older Bass Trail. Although the trail was rough, things went well getting to the bottom of the canyon and getting their equipment across the river. It wasn't until it came time to get the horses across that problems arose. The tram's cage would only hold one horse at a time, plus a person to try to keep the animal calm as the cage swung back and forth on the cable. As the first horse started across, accompanied by Owens's nephew Bill Vaughn, the horse got excited and broke through the front gate, ending up hanging in midair by a rope tied to its halter. The horse's weight caused the cage to swing wildly, and everyone was worried that the cage would come apart, dumping Bill and the horse into the river. The only way to avoid disaster was to sacrifice the dangling horse, so Bill cut the rope, letting the poor animal plunge fifty feet into the river, where it was immediately swept away. For the next trip, the cage was repaired and reinforced, and Bill was able to get the remaining horses across. After getting across the river, the riders had to negotiate a rough trail up Shinumo Creek, which was also in flood stage. During the ascent, the horse carrying the camera equipment that they hoped to use to film their adventures slipped and fell into the creek, destroying some of their film. Fighting the rough trail, they finally emerged on top of the North Rim, where Owens awaited them. The men then had to ride twenty-five miles back to the east to Owens's camp. Due to the flooding, they had been forced to travel fifty miles out of their way and had a once-in-lifetime adventure.[134]

Writer and film producer Rex Beach's party lost a horse after it broke out of the Bass Tram while crossing the Colorado River. *Rex Beech*, Oh Shoot!: Confessions of an Agitated Sportsman, *1921.*

Beach and Stone remained on the North Rim for a month, hunting, roping and filming lions. During their stay, they also had an opportunity to film a bear, which were rather rare on the North Rim. They did not kill the bear, but Owens did something that was rather interesting. When he was in Yellowstone, Uncle Jimmy observed that when Buffalo Jones caught a bear that was raiding camps or being a nuisance, he would rope it and beat it with a stick. In some cases, this punishment seemed to work, as the bear did not get into any more trouble. On the Kaibab, there were not many places for a bear to cause problems, so any bear that Owens caught was most likely just minding its own business. Nevertheless, when Owens caught one, he would follow Jones's example and rope it and beat it with a stick. With the capture of lions and a bear, Beach's party was in high spirits and looked forward to making their return trip down the Bright Angel Trail. However, their hopes were dashed when they were told that the Bright Angel Trail was still flooding, and they would have to return on the horrendous Bass Trail.[135]

Following in Zane Grey's footsteps, another writer, Emerson Hough, also traveled to the Arizona Territory to hunt with Owens. Hough was best known for writing Western stories and historical novels. One of his notable works was *The Story of the Cowboy*, which President Roosevelt highly recommended because of its accuracy of the cowboy's way of life. Another of his best sellers was *The Covered Wagon*, which was made into a movie of the same name, making him one of the first Western authors to have his work made into a movie. In addition to writing novels, Hough worked for *Forest and Stream* magazine. As part of that job, he surveyed the Yellowstone buffalo herd in 1893, when it was estimated that there were five hundred animals. He found fewer than one hundred. After hunting with Owens and seeing the beautiful forest of the North Rim, Hough wrote in the *Saturday Evening Post* that the Kaibab forest should be called the "President's Forest."[136] Other individuals to hunt with Owens included the actors Fred Stone and David Montgomery.

These two actors started out in vaudeville together as the Tin Man and the Scarecrow, respectively, in the 1903 Broadway musical *The Wizard of Oz*. A third author, Hal Evarts, an outdoor and children's author, also hunted with Owens. Owens's clients not only came from all over the United States but also foreign countries. These European hunters were usually very rich and sometimes claimed a little royal blood, such as Lord Teasdale from England. Regardless of their backgrounds or notoriety though, the one thing they all had in common was the desire to see the Grand Canyon and experience the thrills of hunting lions with Uncle Jimmy Owens.

Emerson Hough, novelist and outdoor writer, hunted with Owens and brought nationwide attention to the beauty of the Kaibab by writing several articles in the *Saturday Evening Post*. *The* Critic, *May 1902.*

Of those who hunted with Uncle Jimmy, the best-known person was Teddy Roosevelt. In 1913, Roosevelt, along with his sons nineteen-year-old Archie and fifteen-year-old Quentin and his twenty-year-old nephew Nicholas, joined Owens for a hunt. Originally, Nicholas had made arrangements for the Grand Canyon Transportation Company to guide Roosevelt's party. However, when they reached the Colorado River in the bottom of the Grand Canyon, no one was there to meet them. Fortunately, several cowboys from the Bar Z Cattle Company were crossing the river at the same time and helped Roosevelt cross the river on Rust's tram, which Roosevelt described as a "bully good ride." The next day, the Bar Z men helped the party get to the North Rim, where they met the Grand Canyon Transportation Company men, who were two days late. Roosevelt was irate and told them that he would not need their services. Instead, he went straight to Uncle Jimmy's cabin to hire him for the hunt.[137] Owens immediately agreed and treated them as if they were intended to be his guests. Roosevelt was very impressed with Owens, saying, "A kinder host and a better company in the wild country could not be found." After getting settled in, Roosevelt stayed for twenty days and the boys for two months.[138] Roosevelt did not plan to hunt, since he had taken lions in Colorado, but hoped each of the boys would get a lion. By the time their hunt ended, all three boys, along with Roosevelt, had taken a lion, but not without some scary moments.

Owens often hunted lions by riding along the rim of the Grand Canyon. In most places, there was an upper cliff wall and then a steep bench underneath

Theodore Roosevelt and his family hunted with Owens in 1913. (*From left*): Son Archie, nephew Nicholas, Theodore Roosevelt, Owens, son Quentin and Jesse Cummins. *Grand Canyon National Park Museum Collection, no. 10455.*

before big red cliffs dropped into the depths of the Grand Canyon. From experience, Owens had learned that lions liked to spend their day on the brushy benches and then come up through breaks in the upper cliffs to hunt at night. By hunting along the edge of the canyon, his dogs could find the scent of where a cat had gone over the rim and trail it along the bench until they treed it. This was the technique Owens used on the day Roosevelt and his son Archie had an experience to remember.

The hunting party started out riding through the pines along the rim of the canyon. As they did so, Owens's dogs struck a track and, after trailing it for a short distance, went over the rim and onto the brushy bench underneath. Standing on top of the rim, the hunters listened to the dogs trailing underneath. It wasn't long before they heard the barking become more excited, and they knew the lion was treed. As they looked over the rim, they could see the lion in a big pine tree just above the red cliffs. Owens found a break in the cliffs, and he, Teddy and Archie scrambled down to the tree. Owens told Archie to take his time and make a killing shot, because if the lion struggled, it would slide over the edge and fall thousands of feet into the depths of the canyon. Archie followed Owens's directions and killed the lion instantly.

Since the hunters ended up a long way down the slope, Owens suggested that Archie go back and lead the horses down through a break in the cliff.

Meanwhile, he and Roosevelt would skin the cat. When Archie returned, the lion had been skinned, and the flesh and hide were ready to be tied on Archie's horse and Owens's mule. As the three men started their climb, the horses and mule were having a hard time, scrambling and lunging to keep their footing on the steep slope. This activity caused the saddles carrying the loads to become loose, and they turned under the bellies of the two animals. Archie's horse, spooked by the turned saddle, began to plunge and rear as Archie tried to keep the animal pointed uphill, knowing that if it turned down the slope, it would plunge over the cliff to its death in the canyon far below. Archie was hanging on for dear life, and his dad just hoped that if the horse did go over the cliff, his son would not go with it. With Archie hanging on with all his might, Owens managed to get the saddle loose and the horse settled down. Once the horse was calmed down, it and the mule were both repacked and led to the top of the canyon rim without further trouble. The experience was one Roosevelt would never forget, and as a thank-you, he gave Uncle Jim one of his Winchester rifles embellished with Roosevelt's personal gold-colored plate on the stock. Owens carried the rifle for years, but unfortunately, it was stolen from one of his camps, and he was never able to get it back.[139]

Roosevelt was so impressed, not only with Owens's ability to tree lions but also with the spectacular scenery of the Kaibab Plateau and the Grand Canyon that he recorded it all in his book *A Book-Lover's Holiday in the Open*. Roosevelt hoped that the Grand Canyon Game Preserve, which he created, would someday be made into a National Park like Yellowstone and Yosemite. His wish finally came true on February 26, 1919. Unfortunately, Roosevelt did not live to see it happen. He died on January 6, 1919, fifty-one days before the Grand Canyon became a national park.

The hunting exploits of such people as Roosevelt, Grey and Beach soon made Owens into something of a celebrity to the general public through such books as Grey's *Hunting Lions in the Grand Canyon*,[140] Beach's *Oh, Shoot!: Confessions of an Agitated Sportsman—On the Trail of the Cowardly Cougar*[141] and

Uncle Jimmy with the rifle Roosevelt gave him, bearing Roosevelt's personal brass medallion in the stock. *Grand Canyon National Park Museum Collection, no. 05277.*

Roosevelt's *Book-Lover's Holiday*.[142] Owens and one of his pack burros even became the fictional characters Uncle Jim and Brighty in Marguerite Henry's children's book *Brighty of the Grand Canyon*, complete with an illustration of Beach's horse, or, in her case, a burro, breaking out of the Bass tram.[143]

Henry first learned of Brighty when she read a 1922 *Sunset Magazine* article by Tom McKee, titled "Brighty Free Citizen: How the Sagacious Hermit Donkey of the Grand Canyon Maintained His Liberty for Thirty Years." In the article, McKee described how Brighty, named for Bright Angel Creek, shared his summers on the North Rim between McKee's tourist camp and Owens's cabin in Harvey Meadow and wintered in the depths of the canyon. McKee used the little burro to pack water for his camp, and Owens used him to pack equipment for his hunting camps. He even helped pack supplies on Roosevelt's hunt. Fascinated by McKee's article, Henry traveled from her home in Illinois to the Grand Canyon to learn more about Brighty. While there, she talked to park rangers and local people, which is undoubtedly where she learned about Uncle Jimmy. While at the canyon, she also met Brighty's relatives as she hiked some of the canyon's trails to get a feel for what life was like for a burro in the Grand Canyon.

Even though Henry never met Owens or the real burro Brighty, her book was an instant success and was followed by a film starring Joseph Cotten as game warden Jim Owens. The film was produced by Steve Booth, a television producer, who so loved the Brighty character that he had a bronze statue of the burro cast and gave it to Grand Canyon National Park in 1967. The statue remained on display at the South Rim Visitor Center for ten years before it was removed and put in storage because of a conflict in the park.[144]

Starting in 1968, the Park Service set out to rid the canyon of burros, a nonnative species, by shooting them. Because of this killing of burros in the park, plus other areas throughout the West, people could not understand why the park treated burros as symbols of animals that inhabited the park and were also killing them. The burro controversy became so heated that in 1971, Congress passed the Wild and Free Roaming Horses and Burro Act, which made shooting burros illegal. However, this act did not stop the Park Service, because it had a mandate to protect the park from nonnative species, which superseded the Wild Horse and Burro Act. The public was outraged, and voiced so much opposition to the shooting that the Park Service removed the Brighty statue to try to quell the opposition. The removal of Brighty, however, only made matters worse. People who loved the Brighty story and the statue, started a Bring Brighty Back campaign, which Marguerite Henry

The real burro Brighty of the Grand Canyon (*left*), who packed water for the Wylee Way camp and supplies for Owens. *Grand Canyon National Park Museum Collection, no. 05270.*

supported, and she urged her readers to protest against shooting burros and the removal of the statue.

Due to all of the controversy, the Park Service was finally forced to stop killing burros. With money provided by the Fund for Animals, the Park Service captured and helicoptered most of the remaining burros out of the canyon to a ranch in Texas, where they could be adopted. With the burro conflict resolved, Brighty was brought out of storage in 1980, but this time, the statue was placed at Grand Canyon Lodge on the North Rim, where Brighty originally roamed. Owens probably never dreamed that the little pack burro would cause so much trouble.[145]

All of Owens's guiding, though, was not just to hunt lions. In some instances, people just wanted a guide to show them the Grand Canyon from the North Rim. One significant trip of this type was in 1911, when Owens guided Arizona territorial historian Sharlot Hall around the Kaibab Plateau for four days to let her see what the North Rim looked like.[146] Hall chose to make her trip to the Kaibab by wagon, rather than crossing the canyon, so

Brighty statue, which sparked a lot of controversy for the U.S. Park Service over depicting burros as part of the animal life of the Grand Canyon and then working to eliminate them from the park. *Grand Canyon National Park Museum Collection, no. 05135.*

she could see firsthand what the country north of the canyon looked like. She and guide Al Doyle left Flagstaff on July 23, 1911. They followed the wagon road that most travelers of the day used. The route went first to Tuba City, on the Navajo Indian Reservation, then to Lee's Ferry and finally along the base of the Vermillion Cliffs to Fredonia. She arrived in Fredonia on August 13, twenty-one days after leaving Flagstaff, which shows how difficult it was to get to the North Rim in the early 1900s. She then spent a few days in Fredonia before heading to the North Rim to meet Jimmy Owens.

When she reached his camp, Owens insisted on fixing supper while Hall admired the lion paws and skulls that bordered the ceiling of his cabin and all of the cat claws nailed to the outside.[147] Earlier in the day, Owens had killed a bobcat that he was roasting over the fire. He broke off a piece to eat and offered Sharlot a taste. She gave it a try and said that "she didn't mind it half as much as the first shrimp I ever ate."[148] Serving lion or bobcat meat to his guests was not an uncommon thing for Owens. Roosevelt, during his hunt, mentioned that the only fresh meat they had

Visitors to Owens's cabin were quick to note the hides, skulls and lion claws that covered the walls. *NAU. PH.568.8189.*

was lion meat, which he said "was delicious: quite as good as venison." During the four days Sharlot spent on the North Rim with Owens, she enjoyed the beautiful forest and spectacular views of the canyon from prominent viewpoints between Bright Angel Point and Point Imperial. In fact, she thought the North Rim would be "a lovely place to be buried."[149] Undoubtedly, Owens thought the same thing.

When Sharlot was ready to leave, she thanked Owens for showing her such a wonderful place, and she left with the impression that Uncle Jimmy was one of the few hunters and trappers left from the "old days."[150] Sharlot returned to Fredonia to finish her trip across what is now called the Arizona Strip, recrossed the Colorado River at Gregg's Ferry near present-day Meadview, Arizona, proceeded to Kingman and finally to Flagstaff seventy-two days after she had started. Hall's trip, which covered hundreds of miles in a wagon, was done to raise awareness among Arizona residents of the beautiful country north of the Grand Canyon and to prevent Utah from taking it.

Shortly after the Arizona Territory was created in 1863, it began to lose land. In 1866, the newly formed state of Nevada wanted to get access to the Colorado River. Congress granted this request in 1867, giving Nevada all of the western end of the Arizona Territory. Arizona protested, but Congress was unsympathetic, because Arizona had aligned itself with the Confederacy during the Civil War. Utah, seeing that Nevada was successful in changing its state boundaries, thought it might be able to do the same. Utah argued that since the land north of the Grand Canyon was more accessible and could be developed easier by the people of Utah than Arizona, it should belong to them. Utah made several attempts to gain control of the area starting in 1897.[151] Hall was extremely worried that if the people of Arizona were not made aware of Arizona's treasures north of the Grand Canyon the area would be lost to Utah.[152] When Hall returned from her trip, she wrote about the beauty of the little strip of land that Arizona owned north of the Colorado River in the new state magazine *Arizona*, which later became known as *Arizona Highways*. Her beautiful description of the Kaibab Plateau evidently convinced people to preserve it because when Arizona was granted statehood in 1912 the North Rim was part of it.

In 1919, shortly before Grand Canyon National Park was created, Uncle Jimmy quit his Forest Service job and went into guiding full time, along with his two nephews Bill and Bob Vaughan. By this time, he was well known and had proven his skills as a lion hunter and guide. To advertise his business, he erected a sign at the head of the Bright Angel Creek which read: "Jim Owens Camp, Guiding Tourists and Hunting Parties a Specialty, Cougars Caught to Order."

Owens's timing to go into full-time guiding could not have been better. Hound hunting for lions was becoming a popular sport, and based on Owens's reputation, hunters knew their money would be well spent if they hired him. Also, with the construction of a new road to Wylee Way Camp, a permanent tent camp that could accommodate up to twenty-five tourists at Bright Angel Point, it made the North Rim much more accessible not only to hunters but also tourists.[153] Owens's camp location in Harvey Meadow also made it easy for him to look after his buffalo herd, including his spotted buffalo, Spot, which proved to be a big tourist attraction.[154] Owens continued to operate his guide business into the late 1920s, when his hearing got so poor that he could no longer follow his hounds. By 1927, Uncle Jimmy Owens had caught his last lion.

CHANGING TIMES

A s time went on, Owens saw significant changes on the North Rim. In 1906, Theodore Roosevelt had established the area around the Kaibab Plateau as the Grand Canyon Game Preserve, which brought Owens to the area in 1907 as its first game warden. Then, in 1908, Roosevelt set aside the canyon itself as a national monument. During this time, Owens was free to hunt and kill lions anywhere and was even allowed to shoot wild horses to feed his dogs. All of this changed in 1919, when the canyon and part of the Kaibab Plateau were designated Grand Canyon National Park.

Under Park Service management, Owens found that things were different than when the U.S. Forest Service administered the area. Since Owens worked for the Forest Service, any decisions about where his horses and buffalo were allowed to graze were made at the local level. Under Park Service management, decisions had to go through a chain of command and were made by those Owens called "swivel chair men" in Washington, D.C.[155] A good example of the bureaucratic red tape that Owens had to deal with is demonstrated in his 1921 request to graze eighty head of horses and sixty-four head of buffalo on Nankoweap Pocket and Greenland Plateau (Valhalla Plateau). This permit had to be approved by not only the Grand Canyon Park superintendent, DeWitt Reaburn, but also the director of the National Park Service, Stephen Mather, in Washington, D.C., a process that could take weeks or months.

Another change created by the formation of Grand Canyon National Park began to affect Owens financially. Under park rules, he was not allowed to kill deer and horses to feed his dogs. Instead, he had to buy beef. Understandably, this rule agitated Owens because the lions could eat all the deer they wanted, but his dogs, which protected the deer herd, could not.[156] Due to the increased costs of feeding his dogs, and the Park Service administering some of his favorite hunting areas, Owens resigned from the Forest Service in 1919 and took up guiding people for lions full time. Before that, he had been taking some people on lion hunts, such as Roosevelt and Beech, but now guiding became a full-time job. This change can be seen between the 1910 census, where he listed his occupation as "Game Warden U.S National Forest" and the 1920 census, where he changed his occupation to "hunter trapper."[157] Guiding provided Owens with some income, but as his hearing began to fail and he could no longer take hunting parties on lion hunts, he was forced to find another way to make a living. He decided to go into the tourist business.

By the 1920s, more and more people were finding their way to the North Rim. Some came from Kanab to the north and some from Flagstaff to the south. The southern route crossed the Canyon at Lee's Ferry, or on the Bright Angel Trail. One reason more tourists were finding their way to the North Rim was due to the construction of a better road across the plateau and the creation of an economical camp at Bright Angel Point. By 1913, a road was being built from southern Utah through Fredonia to Jacob's Lake. At the same time, the Forest Service started construction of a road from Jacob's Lake to the North Rim. By today's standards, this road was not much more than an improved wagon road through the forest, but in 1913, it was like a highway. Over time, this road was improved by filling in ruts and washes and eliminating steep grades. Today, the road exists as Highway 67, the primary access road to the North Rim.[158]

With the completion of the Forest Service road, a few hardy individuals began to find their way to the North Rim, but they had to bring their own camping supplies. There were no lodges or cabins on the north side of the canyon similar to El Tovar Lodge on the South Rim. Seeing this problem as an opportunity, an entrepreneur by the name of William Wylie establish a permanent campsite on Bright Angel Point in 1917. Wylie had first employed the concept of a permanent camp in Yellowstone National Park in the 1880s. Wylie Way Camps consisted of tent cabins and a dining tent, which were set up in mid-June and remained in place until around the first of October. Each tent had a wooden floor covered by a rug, a wood-burning stove, some

The construction of a road across the Kaibab Plateau in 1913 made it easier for tourists and hunters to get to Owens's camp in Harvey Meadow but was little more than an old wagon road. *Kaibab National Forest, F223867.*

A Wylie Way camp, similar to this camp in Yellowstone National Park, was established in 1917 at Bright Angel Point as the first tourist camp on the North Rim. *Yellowstone National Park, 02814.*

furniture and a good bed. Campers dined together in the dining tent and were entertained with music, dancing and stories told around the campfire. Wylie's camp could accommodate about twenty people for a price of six dollars per day each. Since Wylie also had a similar camp in Zion National Park, he had his daughter, Elizabeth, run the Grand Canyon camp, along with a summer crew of local teenagers.[159]

With the growing tourist business, Owens saw the potential for guided horseback camping trips for people who wanted to visit some of the more remote and scenic parts of the North Rim, such as Greenland Plateau, Cape Royal, Point Sublime, Tiyo Point and Fossil Point. In April 1921, Owens submitted a plan to the Park Service for a permit to guide parties along the North Rim trails and down the Bright Angel Trail to the Colorado River. In addition, he wanted to establish a summer tent camp on Cape Royal, similar to Wylie's camp, to accommodate fifteen to twenty people at a time.[160] To make his camp distinctly different from Wylie's, he also planned to have some of his permitted buffalo grazing in the area as a tourist attraction.[161] The interesting thing about this plan was that Owens only wanted to take tourists on trail rides. He asked his friend Thomas McKee, the husband of Elizabeth Wylie McKee, to run the camp for him. In a letter to McKee, dated March 24, 1921, asking McKee if he wanted to run the camp, Owens said, "I do not care to feed and house people overnight."[162] In other words, he didn't want to be camped with a bunch of tourists. He only wanted to use his horses and pack animals to get them to the camp and to take them on trail rides, while McKee would be left to run the camp. Why Owens thought McKee would be available to run his camp rather than working with his wife at Wylie Way is not known, but for some reason, McKee never went to work for Owens.

As part of the plan, Uncle Jim also submitted a schedule to the Park Service of what it would cost a person to stay at the camp and go on one of the horseback trips. These trips varied in length, from one to three days, at $5 per day for saddle and pack horses and $5 per day per person for meals and bedding.[163] Thus, if he had twenty people at his camp for three days, he could make $600. Not a bad wage in 1921.

Authorized rates for Trail Trips

From Woolley Cabin on North Rim of Grand Canyon.
1921 Season.

DOWN BRIGHT ANGEL TRAIL TO RIVER:

Three day trip, leave Woolley Cabin at 9:00 a. m. Return
at 5:30 p. m. on third day.
Rates: $5.00 per day for each saddle horse & each pack horse,
5.00 " " per person for meals and bedding.

For parties of less than three persons there is a party charge
of $5.00 per day extra for guide.

GREENLAND PLATEAU AND CAPE ROYAL:

Three day, 60 mile scenic trip, leave Woolley Cabin at 9:00
a. m. Return at 5:30 p. m. on third day.

Rates: $5.00 per day for each saddle horse & each pack horse,
5.00 " " per person for meals and bedding.

For parties of less than three persons there is a party charge
of $5.00 per day extra for guide.

POINT SUBLIME:

Three day, 60 mile scenic trip including Basin Point and Mill
Creek, leave Woolley Cabin at 9:00 a. m. Return at 5:30 p. m. third day.
Rates: $5.00 per day for each saddle horse & each pack horse.
5.00 " " per person for meals and bedding.

For parties of less than three persons there is a party charge
of $5.00 per day extra for guide.

TWO POINT:

One day, 20 mile scenic trip including Gun Sight Point and Vernon
Point.
Rate: $5.00 per day for each horse.

For parties of less than three persons there is a party charge
of $5.00 per day extra for guide.

FOSSIL POINT:

One day, 20 mile scenic trip to double points.
Rate: $5.00 per day for each horse.

For parties of less than three persons there is a party charge
of $5.00 per day extra for guide.

SPECIAL TRIPS:

To Powell Plateau, Swamp Point, South Big Spring, Fish Tail and
other points can be arranged for at same rates as for the regular trips.

Recommended for Approval,
March 8, 1921 at Grand Canyon, Ariz.

D. L. Reahurn
Superintendent.

A 1921 price list for trips and lodging at Owens's proposed pack-in tourist camp. *Grand Canyon National Park Museum Collection, James T. Owens Archives.*

By the spring of 1921, Owens's tourist plan started to come together. The Park Service approved his request to graze sixty-four head of buffalo and eighty head of horses in the park. Unfortunately, that's all it approved. After reviewing Owens's camp plan, the Park Service denied it, not because of the plan itself but because of a Park Service rule that stated, "All privileges must be advertised for and let to the best and most responsible bidder." Unfortunately for Owens, a bid to operate hotels and other facilities in the park had already been awarded to the Fred Harvey Company. Harvey ran the El Tovar Hotel and other tourist operations on the South Rim, but at that time, Fred Harvey had no plans to develop anything on the North Rim. Since Harvey had no current plans, to get around the problem National Park director Mather suggested to Grand Canyon National Park supervisor Reaburn that Owens be granted a temporary permit for the year 1921, "to operate a camp to take care of his trail ride parties." Nothing permanent like corrals or buildings could be built.[164] These limitations, plus only a temporary permit for his tourist plan, apparently was not a suitable arrangement for Owens. He had told Reaburn that he planned to start his camp in June 1921, but there is no record that he ever followed through with his idea.[165]

With his failing hearing making it impossible to hunt and the rejection of his tourist plan, Uncle Jimmy turned his efforts to the only thing he had left that would give him income—his buffalo herd. Counting the buffalo that Buffalo Jones had taken to New Mexico and the twelve calves that the Grand Canyon Cattle Company took to Mexico, Owens was left with a little less than one hundred head. He had park permits to summer graze his buffalo in the park and always had some around his camp in Harvey Meadow for the tourists to see and photograph. However, he needed more area to graze them. Owens wrote his friend Mather a letter, requesting the use of some additional land in the park for his buffalo herd. Mather said he would try to arrange it. In the same letter, Mather also asked Owens if he might like to will his herd to the Park Service. He wrote, "I think it would be a fine thing if you would keep the buffalo during your lifetime and then will the herd with the understanding that it be known as the James T. Owens herd, to the National Park Service of the Department of the Interior and any increase in animals would be given to various towns and cities."[166]

It's interesting to note that Mather thought the buffalo should remain on the North Kaibab because in later years the Park Service wanted to eliminate them because they considered buffalo to be a non-native exotic animal in Arizona.

At the time, it appeared that the Park Service would not inherit the buffalo herd because Owens did not take Mather up on his offer. Instead, in early 1926, he offered his herd of buffalo, except for Spot, to Coconino County, Arizona, for $10,000, with the understanding that the herd would be turned over to the state.[167] The state legislature, however, would not appropriate any money for the purchase. Determined to purchase the herd, a group of sportsmen from the Flagstaff Game Protective Association joined with Coconino County officials to promote the buffalo and raise the needed money through donations.[168] To make people aware of this attempt, four calves were captured and displayed in Flagstaff and Phoenix during the Arizona State Fair "Days of 49" exhibit.[169] This plan, however, failed to raise much money, so the Arizona Game and Fish Department, which wanted to manage the herd as a hunted herd, increased the price of hunting and fishing licenses to pay for the purchase. Unfortunately, this effort raised only $4,000.[170] The game department had to find another way to raise the rest of the money.

The plan that the game department originally developed for the management of the buffalo when it acquired the herd was to not hunt until the herd increased to two hundred animals. With only $4,000, this hunt plan was not an option, since the $6,000 balance owed Owens had to be paid by the end of 1929. During the summer of 1926, the Arizona Game and Fish Department, working with Owens, devised a plan in which fifteen hunters would be allowed to hunt "outlaw buffalo" in House Rock Valley.[171] These outlaw buffalo were fifteen very old bulls that wouldn't stay with the main herd because of being run out by the younger bulls. Basically, the only way Owens could do anything with them was to shoot them himself, which was a difficult chore at his age and would bring him little money. So, why not let the state collect money from hunters and the sale of the meat, which would then be returned to Owens as payment for the herd.

The first buffalo hunt to be held in Arizona attracted a lot of interest. Some 1,500 hunters applied for the fifteen permits, which cost $2.50. The drawing for these permits was held in front of the grandstand at the Arizona State Fair. The hunt commenced on November 23, 1927.[172] Three hunters a day, accompanied by the state game warden and some of his men, were allowed to hunt during the five-day hunt. Each hunter was allowed to keep the head and hide of the animal he killed, plus one hundred pounds of the meat. The remainder of the meat was hauled to Flagstaff and Phoenix by Henry Chambers, who owned Chambers Transfer and Storage Company, where meat was held until it could be sold.[173] In a few days, buffalo meat was up for sale in Phoenix in Bayless Stores and Welnick's Market.[174] The price ranged from $0.50 to $0.80 per pound, depending on the cut. The Game and Fish Department conducted another hunt in 1929 to cull ten more old bulls. All of the proceeds from these hunts were used to pay Owens, and for the first time in twenty-one years, Uncle Jimmy was out of the buffalo business. However, for the Park Service, buffalo management was just getting started.

When Uncle Jimmy and Buffalo Jones first pastured their buffalo in the Grand Canyon Forest Reserve, it was in the area set aside by President Roosevelt in 1906 to protect wild animals. In June 1906, Congress, following up on Roosevelt's intent, passed An Act for the Protection of Wild Animals in the Grand Canyon Forest Reserve. This act named buffalo specifically as a species worthy of protection and took in the entire North Rim of the Grand Canyon.[175] Shortly thereafter, the herd moved itself to House Rock Valley, where it was hunted each year. Due to this hunting pressure, a few buffalo started to seek refuge in the park, which created a conflict between the State of Arizona and the park. The National Park Service classified buffalo as an exotic species, since they were introduced by Owens and Jones. According to the Park Service's definition, a nonnative exotic species was "one that occurred in a given place as the result of direct or indirect, deliberate, or accidental actions by humans, with the result that the manipulated species occurs in a place where it has not evolved with the species native to the place and therefore is not a natural component of the ecological system characteristic of the place."[176]

This definition seemed to fit the Grand Canyon buffalo herd exactly. Since part of the park's mission was to eliminate exotic species, if a buffalo ventured into the park, it could be eliminated. The Park Service, however, never removed any animals, as there were very few that left House Rock Valley.[177]

The big question between Arizona and the park was whether buffalo were non-native or native in Arizona. For many years, the scientific community struggled with this question. Eventually, however, it was proven that buffalo historically did occur in Arizona and New Mexico and even south into Mexico. Spanish explorers mentioned seeing a small buffalo herd in northern Arizona in the mid-1500s, and pictographs of buffalo can be found in Kanab Creek and on the San Francisco Peaks near Flagstaff. Because of these findings, the Park Service had to treat buffalo like other wildlife in the park and could not shoot them indiscriminately.[178]

Using hunting to keep the buffalo herd at approximately one hundred head appeared to work well for many years. The animals seemed content to spend most of their time in House Rock Valley, with only an occasional buffalo venturing into the park. The first buffalo hunts in House Rock Valley were "free ranging" hunts, where hunters, accompanied by a Game and Fish employee, would hunt buffalo like they would deer or elk. As the herd grew, however, more and more hunters were needed to remove enough animals to prevent overgrazing the forage in House Rock Valley. This increase in hunter numbers required more time and effort on the part of Arizona Game and Fish Department personnel. To make it easier for the department to administer the hunt, it was decided that it would be better to corral the buffalo before the hunt, select the animals to be killed and turn the rest back into House Rock Valley. Hunters selected for the hunt would then line up along a fenced area and shoot their animal in what became known as corral hunts.

This type of hunting continued until 1970, when Glendon Swarthout wrote a fictionalized description of the hunt in his book *Bless the Beasts and Children*.[179] The depiction of hunters shooting buffalo in a corral unleashed such a protest that the Game and Fish Department was forced to revert back to free ranging hunts, but this time, hunters were not accompanied by state personnel. Hunters were on their own. With a greater number of hunters pursuing buffalo throughout House Rock Valley, animals were chased through fences that previously stopped them from entering the park and caused them to seek refuge in the higher portions of the Kaibab Plateau, where they were not hunted. Once in the park, they were encouraged to stay by two other factors. First, a prolonged drought in Arizona reduced the forage in House Rock Valley, and second, large wildfires created more forage in the park. The combination of these factors caused the majority of the buffalo to remain in the park, with only a few returning to House Rock Valley. Since the Park Service did not allow hunting, the herd began to grow, and by 2012, it was estimated to number over three hundred head.[180] The Arizona Game and Fish Department, which still managed the herd for the state, estimated that without hunting, the herd would grow by 30 to 50 percent each year. The estimate proved to be correct, as by 2016, the herd was estimated at 600 animals and had the potential to grow to 1,200 to 1,500 in the next ten years.[181]

The Park Service was feeling the changing times just like Uncle Jimmy had in the 1920s. Based on the evidence that buffalo did occur in northern Arizona at one time, the Park Service changed their status from exotic to native species in 2014 and set out to develop a plan to manage buffalo in the park. An interagency group with representatives from Grand Canyon National Park, Arizona Game and Fish Department, U.S. Forest Service,

Today, descendants of Uncle Jimmy's buffalo once again roam the meadows and forests of the North Rim. *National Park Service.*

Bureau of Land Management and Inter-Tribal Buffalo Council started working to develop a buffalo management plan for both inside and outside the park. Since the buffalo herd was increasing rapidly, the first thing the interagency group had to do was address the problem of how to curtail the rapidly increasing numbers. Options considered included capturing and relocating buffalo to other areas and lethal removal.[182] Killing buffalo, however, caused disagreement. The State of Arizona was responsible for the management of wildlife in the state and felt that if any animals were going to be killed, Arizona hunters should have the opportunity to hunt them. The Park Service stated that recreational hunting was not authorized in the park. If buffalo were going to be killed, it would be done by Park Service personnel, contractors or skilled volunteers.[183] Because culling by shooting was controversial, regardless of who did it, the Park Service decided to try to reduce herd numbers by capturing and relocating animals. In September 2019, thirty-one buffalo were herded into corrals, loaded into livestock trailers and relocated on the Quapaw Nation in northeastern Oklahoma, only four hundred miles from where Uncle Jimmy first learned to work with buffalo on the Goodnight Ranch.[184] As herd numbers are brought under control, buffalo will again graze where Owens and Jones first introduced them in 1906, and perhaps the Park Service will take Mather's 1921 suggestion and name the herd the James T. Owens Buffalo Herd.

8

ALL IN A DAY'S WORK

Mountain lions occur in many places in the Southwest, but few places are more rugged than the Kaibab Plateau. As the North Rim is lined with cliffs on the east and west and the massive Grand Canyon on the south, hunting lions there can be a daunting task. When trailing a lion in this country, a hunter soon learns that these cats can go places that man cannot—unless that man was Uncle Jimmy Owens. Jim thought nothing of following lions through the cliffs and over the rim into the Grand Canyon. Once his hounds found a track, he might be on the trail for several days, sleeping on the ground where nightfall overtook him and taking up the hunt the next day. He pursued these big cats in the hot, dry weather of summer and in the ice and snow of winter. His job was to try to eliminate mountain lions, and he took this chore very seriously. Today, it is difficult to imagine what hunting with Uncle Jimmy would have been like. Fortunately for us, some of Owens's friends and people he guided wrote about their experiences and can give us a feeling of what it was like to spend some time with Uncle Jimmy Owens.

Owens was never one to boast about his adventures, although some seem almost unimaginable. On one particular day, Owens and his helper Ed Cox were guiding Lord Teasdale from England. Close to the rim of the canyon, Owens's dogs struck the trail of a lion. When the dogs got close to the cat, the hunters saw it run to the edge of the canyon and jump off. As the two men peeked over the rim, they figured the lion had probably died, but to their surprise, they saw it sitting in a big pine tree about thirty feet below

Tiyo Point, like other areas on the North Rim, has many levels of cliffs and ledges, making pursuing lions dangerous. *Grand Canyon National Park Museum Collection, no. 04320.*

them. Beyond the lion was nothing, as the cliff on which the pine tree grew dropped several thousand feet into the canyon. It appeared the tree was as far as the lion could go. But this wasn't the case. When the lion saw Owens, it jumped out of the tree and onto a small ledge and ran out of sight. Lord Teasdale remarked to Owens, "That is the last we'll see of that beast," to which Owens replied, "Oh no, he's as good as dead right now."

As Teasdale watched, Owens got out a rope and tied it around his waist. He then had Cox lower him fifty feet over the cliff to the ledge below. Once on the ledge, Jim had Ed tie the rope around each dog and lower them, one at a time, to where he stood. As soon as each dog was untied, they took off after the cat, with Owens right behind them. The dogs eventually put the cat up another tree, and Owens shot it. After skinning the cat, he returned to the rope and had Ed pull the hide and the dogs back onto the rim. Owens then started to pull himself back up the cliff, which was nothing out of the ordinary for him, but Teasdale was astounded—so much so that there are probably no pictures of this feat because Teasdale was so unnerved by seeing Owens hanging by a rope on the side of the Grand Canyon that he forgot to take any pictures.[185]

Another instance of a hunter not believing what Owens would do was when he had a guest who doubted Uncle Jim's statement that "he would climb a tree and rope a lion." This hunter was made a believer, however, when they treed a lion. As Owens began to climb the tree with a rope in his hand, for some reason, the hunter got scared and went back to camp. Owens proved his point by proceeding to rope and tie the lion by himself and brought it back to camp for the hunter to see that he could really catch a lion alive by himself.[186]

Owens's dogs didn't always put lions up trees. They might bay them on a ledge or, in some instances, run them into a cave. The latter situation could be very dangerous. Although lions occasionally attack humans, this is very

Having a hound bay a lion on a dangerous cliff was a common event for Owens. *Photo by H. Shaw.*

rare. However, if they are cornered, like in a cave, they might attack a person out of self-defense. Owens knew this and thought crawling in a cave with a lion was probably a foolhardy thing to do, but he did it anyway. Using a pine knot that was full of pitch, he would light it on fire and crawl into the cave to shoot the lion. In one particular instance, he followed a lion fifty feet back into a deep cave. He hoped to get close enough to kill the animal quickly, but when he fired, instead of dying, the cat charged him. Owens immediately proceeded to empty his gun before killing the lion. If his gun had jammed or he hadn't reacted quickly, the lion probably would have, at the least, scratched him severely or killed him.[187]

When Uncle Jimmy was hunting, he always carried a .30-.30 rifle and an old .45 pistol. The pistol came in handy, especially when he was climbing around on cliffs and ledges and needed to hang on with both hands. There were instances, however, where neither weapon fit the situation. One such case was when he and Bill Mace, a forest ranger, were hunting near Saddle Mountain on the southeast side of the Kaibab Plateau. At times, when Owens was going to make extended trips into the more remote areas of the plateau, one of the forest rangers would accompany him in case he got hurt. This particular trip was going to take about a month. In cases of prolonged hunts like this, Owens would also take several pack horses or burros to carry his food and camp. In fact, pictures of him with his pack burros might be where Marguerite Henry got the idea for her book *Brighty of the Grand Canyon.*

Uncle Jim and Bill set out from Ryan Station and headed for Saddle Mountain, which was a couple of days ride. As they started up the side of the mountain, Mace caught some movement out of the corner of his eye. When he looked closely, he realized there was not just one but three lions about 250 yards away. Bill jumped off his horse and fired at the lions but missed. About the same time, the hounds crossed the fresh track and set off after the cats. The tracks were so fresh that the dogs tore after the lions as fast as they could run, leaving Owens and Mace far behind. When they finally caught up with the dogs, they had one of the lions treed in a pinyon pine that grew on the edge of a 100-foot-deep steep-sided canyon. From where the two stood, Bill could see the lion, but Owens couldn't, so he told Bill to shoot it. When Bill fired, the lion tumbled over the cliff and into the canyon, with the hounds and Uncle Jim right behind. Bill hurried to the edge of the cliff to see what was going on at the bottom of the canyon. Somehow, Uncle Jim had reached the bottom of the canyon as quickly as the dogs, and there he stood with a knife in his hand. The lion was dead, but if Bill had not made a killing shot, there was a chance the cat could hurt or kill one of the dogs. In such a situation, Owens didn't dare shoot the cat, for fear that he might hit a dog, but he was prepared to try to kill the cat with his knife if he had to. Using his knife in this situation might cause Owens to get severely injured, but he was willing to take the risk to protect his dogs.[188]

One really gets a feel for what it was like to try to follow the hounds when hearing about another hunt when Jim was accompanied by Bill Mace. This hunt occurred in the late winter, with deep snow drifts on the north slopes. Uncle Jimmy and Bill were camped near Big Saddle, and as was always the case when they were hunting, they were up before daylight. As dawn broke, the two men started up Little Mountain, and at about sunup, the hounds smelled the tracks of a lion, probably from the night before. Because the track was old, the dogs had difficulty following, and Owens and Mace were able to stay with them. After several hours, the scent slowly became fresher, and the dogs were able to follow the lion more quickly. The cat and the dogs had no trouble running on top of the snow, but the hunters soon fell far behind, as the drifts made it difficult for the horses. All the hunters could do was follow the barking of the hounds. At about two o'clock in the afternoon, the dogs finally overtook the lion and treed it. Unfortunately, as the hunters came into sight, the cat jumped out of the tree, and the hunt started all over again. This pattern continued for several hours, with the dogs treeing the lion, Owens and Mace catching up and the lion jumping out of the tree and running off. Each time, after the lion jumped and ran, the hunters were left far behind and again could only follow the dogs by sound.

As late afternoon approached, the wind picked up, and Owens lost the barking of the dogs altogether. In an effort to find the dogs, the hunters split up, each riding to a high spot where they might be able to hear them. Uncle Jim was the one to finally find them. As before, the dogs had the cat treed, but again, the lion jumped out before Owens could shoot. As it hit the ground, the lion headed straight for Bill Mace, who said, "I saw him

Along with baying lions on cliffs, ledges and caves, Owens's hounds often put them up a tree. *Photo by Zane Grey.*

coming. I thought all the time my horse was about to give out, and I knew I was. But when the horse saw the race, he came to life right now." The lion and dogs raced past Mace and his terrified horse and ran about another half mile before treeing again. This time, the lion finally stayed in the tree, where Mace shot it. It was dark by the time they got the lion skinned and headed for home. As they rode toward camp, Bill told Owens, "Worn out horses, worn out dogs, ten miles to go through a foot of snow to camp, but my, what an exciting chase."[189] Owens and Mace had been up since before daylight until well after dark and had ridden over twenty miles through the snow. This alone would be enough for anyone but not Uncle Jimmy. The next day, he was up before daylight, preparing to hunt another lion.[190]

All of Uncle Jim's adventures did not have to do with cliffs, caves and lions. In one instance, his daring saved a life. In the summer of 1911, Owens had part of his buffalo herd grazing by his cabin near Harvey Meadow, where he could watch over them. At the time, a party of tourists was camped at the far end of the meadow. Owens had warned them that if the buffalo came by, they should stay in their camp until the herd passed and to not do anything to excite them. One afternoon, a group of about twenty-five buffalo came down the meadow on their way to Bright Angel Spring just as two young girls from the camp decided to take a walk. In the herd was a cow that had given Owens trouble whenever he moved the herd. He described the cow as "right down ornery." Only a short time before, she had gored and killed one of Owens's pack animals. At about the time the herd passed Jim's cabin, one of the girls opened and closed an umbrella several times, as if to scare the buffalo away. The umbrella caused the buffalo to start running, not away from the girls but toward them. Owens, hearing the commotion, stepped out of his cabin in time to see the old cow with her head lowered charging at one of the girls. Jim quickly picked up a piece of firewood and started running and hollering straight toward the cow. As he got close, he hit her on the nose with the firewood. This blow turned her just enough to miss him and the girl. If Owens had not risked his life to turn the buffalo, you can imagine what would have happened. At least, the little girl would have been trampled by the old cow or, at worst, gored and thrown into the air like a ragdoll. Uncle Jim, though, was not one to brag or take credit for saving the girl. To him it was just "all in a day's work."[191]

9

THE SEARCH FOR UNCLE JIMMY

With the selling of his buffalo and his health failing, Owens was forced to leave his beloved North Rim. To take care of him, his nephew John Cox moved Uncle Jimmy to his home in Afton, New Mexico, a small railroad stop on the Union Pacific line. Cox worked for the Union Pacific Railroad and evidently was able to arrange a trip back to Texas for a reunion with Owens's good friend Charles Goodnight. While there, Owens had a formal portrait taken with him dressed in a suit and tie. This was probably the first time Owens had dressed in anything other than jeans, a wool shirt and his old beat-up hat in over eighty years.[192]

Undoubtedly, during his visit, Owens spent a lot of time telling Goodnight about his buffalo herd and the hardships and dangers of hunting mountain lions on the North Rim. Owens also probably took time to tell Goodnight of the beautiful things he had seen—the spectacular views of the Grand Canyon from the many prominent points on the North Rim and Thunder River, which burst out of the side of the canyon where there was no other water. He certainly would have told Goodnight about the wildlife—the little white-tailed Kaibab squirrels, the wild turkeys and blue grouse and, of course, all of the deer. During their conversations, he would have mentioned the famous people he had met, such as Teddy Roosevelt, Zane Grey and Emerson Hough, along with the hundreds of visitors to the North Rim who called him Uncle Jimmy.[193]

On his return to New Mexico, Uncle Jim continued to live with his nephew. It was while living in Afton that he was diagnosed with heart disease and finally died of a heart attack on May 11, 1936.[194] However, at this point, the story doesn't end. His final resting place became a mystery. Where was Uncle Jimmy buried?

Since Owens's last known residence was in Afton, New Mexico, it seemed logical that he might be buried there. A visit to Afton, however, proved that was not the case. Not only was there no cemetery in Afton, but there wasn't even a town. All that remained were a few boards marking where the town had been. Since Afton was just a small town on the Union Pacific Railroad, it probably outlived its usefulness along the company's main line. Records showed that the Afton Post Office closed in 1941, and the town probably became a ghost town shortly thereafter.[195]

Portrait of Owens taken when he returned to Texas for a final visit. *Leon Cox.*

The next cemetery searched was in Fredonia, Arizona. This was the closest cemetery to Owens's beloved Kaibab, and perhaps he had requested to be buried there. Unfortunately, a check of headstones revealed nothing. While in Fredonia, a check also was made with the Pratt family, since Owens spent a lot of time with them when he wasn't hunting on the plateau. The only Pratt still living who knew Owens was a woman who was just a young child when Owens was alive. She remembered that Uncle Jimmy "just sort of disappeared," the way some old people do in youngsters' memories, but she had no idea where he might be buried.

When nothing was found in Afton or Fredonia, an electronic search was widened to take in a lot of the cemeteries in southern Utah and northern Arizona. That search also failed to find his grave. Since the graveyard searches were proving unsuccessful, an electronic search for his obituary was undertaken in hopes that it might tell where he was buried. After much searching, his obituary was finally discovered in the *El Paso Herald Post* in El Paso, Texas. It stated that Owens was buried in the Las Cruces, New Mexico cemetery, but the question was which one, since there were three. To make sure that his grave wasn't missed, an electronic search of gravestones was made of all the various Las Cruces cemeteries. Nothing was found. What had happened to Uncle Jimmy?

To try to solve this mystery, a request was made to obtain his death certificate from the New Mexico Bureau of Public Health in hopes it might show where

Owens's death certificate, stating that he was one hundred years old, an age that appears to be false. *State of New Mexico Bureau of Public Health.*

he was buried. And it did. The death certificate showed that Owens was buried in the Masonic Cemetery in Las Cruces. If this was the case, why had the gravestone search failed to show him buried there? To discover how the gravestone had been missed, contact was made with the cemetery personnel.

CEMETERY RECORD—Aztec Lodge No. 3, A. F. & A. M.

Name of Purchaser: J. R. Cox   Address: Afton, N.M.

Reservations: Sec........., Bl............., Lots............

Remarks:

Record of Burial	Relation of Deceased to Lot Owner		DATE	ITEM	DR.	CR.
Name of Deceased James T. Owens		Married Single Widow-er	1936 May	11 1 Grave Permit #290	40	
Date of Birth April 10, 1836 Place of Birth						
Father's Name and Address		Living Deceased				
Mother's Name and Address		Living Deceased	" 15	By Cash R#187		10
Date of Death May 11, 1936 Date of Burial			July 24	By Cash R#263		20
Cause of Death Senility						
Undertaker Graham Mort. Buried in Sec...5... Bl5... Lot 22			Aug 28	By Cash R 210		10

Record of Burial	Relation of Deceased to Lot Owner	
Name of Deceased		Married Single Widow-er
Date of Birth Place of Birth		
Father's Name and Address		
Mother's Name and Address		
Date of Death		
Cause of Death		
Undertaker		

Permit 290

Deceased James T. Owens.

Purchaser J. R. Cox. Afton, N. Mex.

Record of Burial

Name of Deceased

Date of Birth

Father's Name and Address

Mother's Name and Address

Date of Death

Cause of Death

Undertaker

Sec 5 R. 5 Gr. 22

20.00 Cash July 23/36. Balance 10.00

JAMES T. OWENS
"UNCLE JIMMY"
? – Died MAY 11, 1936

Above: Las Cruces New Mexico Masonic Cemetery record showing Owens buried in section 5 grave 22, but no tombstone was found at the grave. *Masonic Cemetery, Las Cruces New Mexico.*

Left: Uncle Jimmy's tombstone was dedicated on November 16, 2013. *Photo by H. Shaw.*

A search of the files revealed that it had a burial record showing that a James T. Owens was buried in Section 5 Grave 22. However, on locating this plot, it was discovered that there was no gravestone marking his grave. Uncle Jimmy Owens had ended up buried in an unmarked grave, far from his beloved North Rim of the Grand Canyon.[196] To rectify the situation, a gravestone was purchased. The stone shows when Owens died, but since his birth date was in doubt, just a question mark replaces a normal date of birth. The stone also has a picture of Owens on his horse taken on the North Rim. At 11:00 a.m. on Saturday, November 16, 2013, the stone was officially dedicated by a group of history lovers, some of whom had helped locate his grave. Uncle Jimmy Owens's story had finally come to an end.

AFTERWORD

The telling of Uncle Jimmy Owens's story has been a long trek of some ten years. Along the way, I have met many people, searched hundreds of records and viewed dozens of old photos and documents. As I proceeded to write about his life, it became obvious that without knowing Owens's final resting place, the story remained unfinished. As I searched one cemetery after another, to no avail, I thought I might never finish this book. It was only when I accidently stumbled on the small obituary in the El Paso newspaper that listed him as being buried in Las Cruces, New Mexico, that I finally found him, or so I thought. Fortunately, the Masonic Cemetery had the record of his burial plot but no information on a headstone. Had it been made out of wood and simply deteriorated over the years, or had one never been purchased? In either case, for a man who had been such a prominent figure in the history of the North Rim, not having a gravestone to mark his final resting place seemed inappropriate. Owens deserved a gravestone. The problem was how to pay for it. Since I had learned about Uncle Jimmy through my work with the Arizona Game and Fish Department, I knew that other past and present employees would also know of Owens. I contacted some of them to see if any would like to donate a few dollars. The response was overwhelming. Within days, there was enough money to buy a beautiful pictured gravestone and have it placed in the cemetery. With the stone's dedication in 2013, my journey to tell Uncle Jimmy's story was complete.

NOTES

Introduction

1. R. Moore and K. Witt, *The Grand Canyon: An Encyclopedia of Geography, History, and Culture* (Santa Barbara, CA: ABC-CILO, LLC, 2018).
2. William M. Mace, *Uncle Jim Owens: Master Cougar Killer of the Kaibab* in James T. Owens Papers, Grand Canyon National Park Archives.
3. B. Swapp, untitled paper in James T. Owens Papers, Grand Canyon National Park Archives.
4. Adrian Forsyth, *Mammals of North America* (Camden East, ON: Camden House, 1985).
5. John P. Russo, *The North Kaibab Deer Herd: Its History, Problems, and Management* (Phoenix: Arizona Game and Fish Department, 1970).
6. Ibid.
7. James Owens, "Government Hunter No. 1: High Spots in the Life of Uncle Jim Owens," *Field and Stream*, May 1937.

Chapter 1

8. 1910 Census, Coconino County, Arizona, U.S. Census Bureau.
9. Theodore Roosevelt, *A Book-Lover's Holiday in the Open: A Cougar Hunt on the Rim of the Grand Canyon* (New York: Charles Scribner's Sons, 1916).
10. "100-Year Old Dies at Afton, N.M.," *El Paso Herold Post*, May 12, 1936.

11. 1930 Census, Coconino County, Arizona, U.S. Census Bureau.

12. 1910 Census, Coconino County.

13. 1930 Census, Coconino County.

14. Annie Dyer Nunn to Lou Garrison, May 16, 1952, Letter in James T. Owens Papers, Grand Canyon National Park Archives.

15. Armstrong County Historical Society, *James (Uncle Jimmy Owens): A Collection of Memories: A History of Armstrong County, 1876–1865* (Denton: University of North Texas, 1965).

16. 1930 Census, Coconino County.

17. Leon Cox to author, personal communication, November 2013.

18. James T. Owens Certificate of Death, May 11, 1936, New Mexico Office of Vital Records and Health Statistics.

19. Leon Cox to author; Andrew C. Isenberg, *The Destruction of the Bison* (New York: Cambridge University Press, 2000).

20. Annie Dyer Nunn to Lou Garrison.

21. S. McLachlan and C. Rivers, eds, *Legends of the West: The History of the James-Younger Gang* (Scotts Valley, CA: Create Space Independent Publishing, 2015).

22. H. Allen Anderson, "Goodnight Ranch," Handbook of Texas, Texas State Historical Association, http//www.tshaonline.org.

23. Annie Dyer Nunn, "Uncle Jim Owens," *Amarillo Sunday News and Globe*, May 17, 1926.

24. Ibid.

25. David A. Dary, *The Buffalo Book: The Full Saga of the American Animal* (Athens: Swallow Press/Ohio University Press, 1974).

26. Robert Easton and Mackenzie Brown, *Lord of Beasts: A Saga of Buffalo Jones* (Tucson: University of Arizona Press, 1961).

27. Ibid.

28. Nunn, "Uncle Jim Owens."

29. Dary, *Buffalo Book.*

Chapter 2

30. Dary, *Buffalo Book.*

31. Ibid.

32. Isenberg, *Destruction of the Bison.*

33. Easton and Brown, *Lord of Beasts.*

34. James T. Owens, Pay Records for Owens, J.T. as Buffalo Keeper for Yellowstone National Park, 12/28/04–1/10/06, James T. Owens Papers, Yellowstone National Park Archives.

35. Isenberg, *Destruction of the Bison*.

36. James T. Owens, Pay Records.

37. L. Barsness, *Heads, Hides & Horns: The Complete Buffalo Book* (Fort Worth: Texas Christian University Press, 1985).

38. James T. Owens, Pay Records.

39. Darrin Lunde, *The Naturalist: Theodore Roosevelt* (New York: Crown Publishers, 2016).

40. James T. Owens, Pay Records.

41. Lunde, *Naturalist*.

42. Theodore Roosevelt, *Outdoor Pastimes of an American Hunter* (New York: Charles Scribner's Sons, 1905); John Burroughs, "Camping with President, Theodore Roosevelt," *Atlantic*, May 1906.

43. Owens, "Government Hunter No. 1."

44. Charles M. Russell, *Arizona Nights*, 1905, watercolor, McClure Company, New York.

Chapter 3

45. Dary, *Buffalo Book*.

46. Ibid.

47. Ibid.

48. Barsness, *Heads, Hides & Horns*.

49. Ibid.

50. Dary, *Buffalo Book*.

51. Ibid.

52. Douglas Brinkley, *The Wilderness Warrior: Theodore Roosevelt and the Crusade for America* (New York: HarperCollins, 2009).

53. Easton and Brown, *Lord of Beasts*.

54. Ibid.

55. Christian C. Young, *In the Absence of Predators* (Lincoln: University of Nebraska Press, 2002).

56. Easton and Brown, *Lord of Beasts*.

57. Brinkley, *Wilderness Warrior*; Young, *In the Absence of Predators*.

58. James T. Owens, Pay Records.

59. Easton and Brown, *Lord of Beasts*.

60. Barsness, *Heads, Hides & Horns*.

61. Dary, *Buffalo Book*.

62. Easton and Brown, *Lord of Beasts*.

63. Ibid.

64. Ibid.

65. Dary, *Buffalo Book*.

66. Easton and Brown, *Lord of Beasts*.

Chapter 4

67. Owens, "Government Hunter No. 1."

68. Ibid.

69. Brinkley, *Wilderness Warrior*.

70. Young, *In the Absence of Predators*.

71. Ibid.

72. D.E. Brown, ed., *Arizona Wildlife: The Territorial Years 1863–1912* (Phoenix: Arizona Game and Fish Department, 2009).

73. Owens, "Government Hunter No. 1."

74. William M. Mace, "Uncle Jim Owens: Master Cougar Killer of the Kaibab," James T. Owens Papers, Grand Canyon National Park Archives.

75. Ibid.

76. Ibid.

77. Ibid.

78. Cathy Viele, "Uncle Jimmy Owens: Canyon Lion Hunter," Northland Back Pages, *Northlander*, 1979.

79. Mace, "Uncle Jim Owens."

80. Owens, "Government Hunter No. 1."

81. Ibid.

82. Mace, "Uncle Jim Owens."

83. Owens, "Government Hunter No. 1."

84. Michel F. Anderson, *Living on the Edge* (Grand Canyon, AZ: Grand Canyon Association, 1998).

85. Ibid.

86. Young, *In the Absence of Predators*.

87. Rowland W. Rider, *Sixshooters and Sagebrush* (Provo, UT: Brigham Young University Press 1979).

88. Young, *In the Absence of Predators*.

89. Ibid.

90. Ibid.
91. Zane Grey, *Roping Lions in the Grand Canyon* (New York: Grosset and Dunlap, 1924); Roosevelt, *Booklover's Holiday*.
92. Young, *In the Absence of Predators*.
93. Ibid.
94. Aldo Leopold, *Game Management* (New York: Charles Scribner's Sons, 1933).
95. Ron Smith to author, personal communication, June 2015.
96. Harley Shaw to author, personal communication, June 2018.
97. Leopold, *Game Management*.
98. Young, *In the Absence of Predators*.

Chapter 5

99. John P. Russo, *The North Kaibab Deer Herd: Its History, Problems, and Management* (Phoenix: Arizona Game and Fish Department, 1970).
100. Brinkley, *Wilderness Warrior*.
101. Russo, *North Kaibab Deer Herd*.
102. Brinkley, *Wilderness Warrior*.
103. Russo, *North Kaibab Deer Herd*.
104. James B. Trefethen, "The Terrible Lesson of the Kaibab," *National Wildlife*, June–July 1967; D.I. Rassmussen, "Biotic Communities of Kaibab Plateau, Arizona," *Ecological Monographs* 11, no. 3 (1941): 236–43.
105. Young, *In the Absence of Predators*.
106. Ibid.
107. Trefethen, "Terrible Lesson"; Young, *In the Absence of Predators*.
108. Trefethen, "Terrible Lesson."
109. Ibid.
110. Russo, *North Kaibab Deer Herd*.
111. Young, *In the Absence of Predators*.
112. Trefethen, "Terrible Lesson."
113. Russo, *North Kaibab Deer Herd*.
114. Wendell G. Swank, "History of the Kaibab Deer Herd Beginning to 1968" (paper presentation, Deer/Elk Workshop, Rio Rico, AZ, 1997).
115. Russo, *North Kaibab Deer Herd*.
116. Trefethen, "Terrible Lesson."
117. Young, *In the Absence of Predators*.
118. Russo, *North Kaibab Deer Herd*.

119. Todd R. Berger, *It Happened at the Grand Canyon*, 2nd ed. (Billings, MT: TwoDot Publishing, 1968).

120. Jack Fuss, "The Great Kaibab Deer Drive," *Coconino Sun*, December 19, 1924.

121. Trefethen, "Terrible Lesson"; Fuss, "Great Kaibab Deer Drive."

122. Zane Grey, *The Deer Stalker* (New York: HarperCollins, 1949).

123. Young, *In the Absence of Predators*.

124. Fuss, "Great Kaibab Deer Drive."

125. Tom Britt to author, personal communication, April 2018.

Chapter 6

126. Zane Grey, *Roping Lions*.

127. Ibid.

128. Owens, "Government Hunter No. 1."

129. Grey, *Roping Lions*.

130. Owens, "Government Hunter No. 1."

131. Swapp, untitled paper, James T. Owens Papers.

132. Frederick H. Swanson, *David Rust: A Life in the Canyons* (Salt Lake City: University of Utah Press, 2007).

133. Owens, "Government Hunter No. 1."

134. Rex E. Beach, *Oh, Shoot!: Confessions of an Agitated Sportsman* (New York: Harper and Brothers, 1921).

135. Ibid.

136. Swanson, *David Rust*.

137. Roosevelt, *Book-Lover's Holiday*.

138. Owens, "Government Hunter No. 1."

139. Roosevelt, *Book-Lover's Holiday*.

140. Grey, *Roping Lions*.

141. Beach, *Oh, Shoot*.

142. Roosevelt, *Book-Lover's Holiday*.

143. Marguerite Henry, *Brighty of the Grand Canyon* (Chicago: Rand McNally, 1953).

144. Erin V. Rheenen, *The Life and Times of Brighty, the Grand Canyon's Most Legendary Burro* (Brooklyn, NY: Atlas Obscura, 2018).

145. Ibid.

146. C.G. Crampton, ed., *Sharlot Hall on the Arizona Strip* (Flagstaff, AZ: Northland Press, 1975).

147. Anderson, *Living on the Edge*.

148. Crampton, *Sharlot Hall*.

149. Ibid.

150. Ibid.

151. Mark Stein, *How the States Got Their Shapes* (New York: HarperCollins, 2008).

152. Crampton, *Sharlot Hall*.

153. Beach, *Oh, Shoot*.

154. Owens, "Government Hunter No. 1."

Chapter 7

155. Thomas McKee H. to Mr. Carlson, June 30, 1951, James T. Owens Papers, Grand Canyon National Park Archives.

156. Ibid.

157. 1920 Census, Coconino County, Arizona, U.S Census Bureau.

158. Swanson, *David Rust*.

159. Sarah B. Gerke, *Wylie Way Camps: Nature, Culture and History of the Grand Canyon* (Tempe: Arizona State University, 2020).

160. James Owens, "Unpublished Trip and Lodging Rates for Owens' Proposed Camp and Guide Service for 1921 Summer Season," James T. Owens Papers, Grand Canyon National Park Archives.

161. Thomas McKee H. to Mr. Carlson.

162. James Owens to Thomas McKee, March 24, 1921, James T. Owens Papers, Grand Canyon National Park Archives.

163. Owens, "Unpublished Trip."

164. Stephen Mather to James Owens, April 23, 1921, James T. Owens Papers, Grand Canyon National Park Archives.

165. James Owens to DeWitt Reaburn, March 12, 1921, James T. Owens Papers, Grand Canyon National Park Archives.

166. Stephen Mather to James Owens, October 28, 1921, James T. Owens Papers, Grand Canyon National Park Archies.

167. "Arizona Buffalo Herd Optioned by Coconino County," *Arizona Republic*, April 2, 1926.

168. "State and County Officials Expect to Launch Campaign for Funds with Which to Give Arizona 100 Buffalo," *Arizona Republic*, July 21, 1926.

169. "Buffalo Calves of Owens' Herd to Be Exhibited," *Arizona Republic*, June 27, 1926.

170. "Fifteen Given Permit to Take Part in Chase," *Arizona Republic*, November 23, 1927.

171. Ibid.

172. Ibid.

173. Ibid.

174. "The Big Feed Is on Today," *Arizona Republic*, December 13, 1927; "Five Thousand Pounds of State Buffalo Meat to Be Placed on Sale in Phoenix Stores Today," *Arizona Republic*, December 13, 1927.

175. "Grand Canyon National Park Bison Management Plan/Environmental Impact Statement—Updated April 25, 2014," Grand Canyon National Park, http://www.Nwf:org.

176. John G. Dennis, "National Park Service Management Policies for the National Park System: The National Park Services Management Policy in the 21st Century, Vol. 16, No. 3," United States Department of Interior, 2006.

177. "Grand Canyon National Park Bison."

178. Ibid.

179. Glendon Swarthout, *Bless the Beasts and Children* (New York: Simon and Schuster, 1970).

180. "Grand Canyon National Park Bison."

181. Ibid.

182. Ibid.

183. Ibid.

184. Debra U. Krol, "First Group of Bison Make the Move from the Grand Canyon to Oklahoma," *Arizona Republic*, September 24, 2019.

Chapter 8

185. Owens, "Government Hunter No. 1."

186. Swapp, untitled paper.

187. Owens, "Government Hunter No. 1."

188. Mace, *Uncle Jim Owens*.

189. Ibid.

190. Ibid.

191. Ibid.

Chapter 9

192. Annie Dyer Nunn, "He Returns as a Famous Man," *Amarillo Sunday News and Globe*, 1927

193. Owens, "Government Hunter No. 1."

194. Certificate of Death, James Thos Owens, New Mexico Bureau of Public Health, 1936.

195. "Afton New Mexico," Ghost Towns, http://ghosttowns.com.

196. James T. Owens Burial Record, Masonic Cemetery, Las Cruces, New Mexico.

INDEX

ABOUT THE AUTHOR

Albert "Al" LeCount is a professional wildlife biologist. He grew up in the state of Washington and received a bachelor of science degree in wildlife biology from Washington State University in 1963 and a master's of science in wildlife management from the University of Arizona in 1970. He worked for the Arizona Game and Fish Department for thirty years, first as a wildlife manager and then as a research biologist. During his thirty years with Arizona, he conducted research on mule deer, mountain lions and bears, the latter of which he studied for over twenty years. Al has published professional papers on his bear work in the *Journal of Wildlife Management*, *Journal of Wildlife Disease*, *Western Journal of Applied Forestry* and *Ursus*. He has published over a dozen popular articles in *Arizona Wildlife Views* and *Falcon Magazine* and has authored chapters for several Arizona Wildlife Federation publications. Over his thirty years with the Arizona Game and Fish Department, he has also presented numerous scientific papers at professional meetings, and in 1985, he received the Arizona governor's Wildlife Conservationist of the Year Award.

Al has conducted black bear workshops for professionals in other states, such as Colorado, Utah and New Mexico. He has done consulting work for Big Bend and Mesa Verde National Parks, and in 1983, he received a Fulbright scholarship to help biologists in Croatia initiate a brown bear research program. He is a past president of the International Bear Association and, in 1983, hosted the sixth International Conference on Bear Research and Management at the Grand Canyon.

In addition to his research, Al has given his time to help Arizona teachers learn how to incorporate wildlife into their curriculum. From 1989 until 1995, he taught a summer class at Northern Arizona University, titled Wildlife for Educators. In addition, he has taught weekend teacher workshops through the Project Wild program. For his efforts to help educators, he was awarded the Arizona Association for Learning in and about the Environment's Lifetime Achievement Award in 1990. In 1976, as a bicentennial project, Al helped the people of Tonto Basin, Arizona, research and record the history of their small community by writing and editing *The History of Tonto*.

On his retirement from the Arizona Game and Fish Department, Al took a job as associate professor of wildlife at Hocking College in southeast Ohio. There, he taught a variety of classes on wildlife management and techniques and coordinated the wildlife program. In 2004, he received Hocking College's award for Excellence in Teaching. While at Hocking College, he also contracted research work with the Ohio Division of Wildlife on Allegheny woodrats and, after his retirement in 2011, volunteered to work on a bobcat project in Ohio. In 2018, Al and his wife, Cheryl Mollohan, returned to Arizona to pursue new wildlife volunteer and contract opportunities.

Visit us at
www.historypress.com

Printed in the USA
CPSIA information can be obtained
at www.ICGtesting.com
LVHW051242261023
761548LV00010B/76